Introduction

The reason for telling my story began one sunny dá dog when my path crossed with a neighbour who commented on a visit I had recently taken to Canada.

She had seen something about it on TV and read a small article in a newspaper and wanted to know more.

I told her a small part of what I had encountered, which had been very emotional.

Before walking on, she said "I have known you for years "It just goes to show you meet people who seem ordinary every day, but you never know what's gone on in their life", then with a "Goodbye Bob!`` She left.

Her comment left me thinking deeply about the life I and my brothers had endured.

I carried on walking my dog, then from across the street another neighbour shouted over to me, "I see you have had your five minutes of fame".

I presumed she had seen the TV report explaining why after 44 years I had returned to Canada.

I felt it was an unjust comment, without saying a word I turned my gaze away from her and carried on walking my dog, at the same time thinking how one neighbour's words were so genuine and kind, the second neighbour I can only say, not so nice.

Within my story, you will read of a tragedy in December 1957 that devastated my family. That life-changing moment in time was unavoidable. What happened after was unforgivable.

My book title Wounded Souls is what many people become at some stage in their life, for I it was at the age of seven and just at the start of my understanding of the importance of family.

Within the pages of my story, you may notice the huge distances in miles, and the decade's in-between news reports.

It was reported in 1957 by several Canadian and English newspapers, also documented by BBC, and Canadian television.

Still bringing interest it was revisited 44 years later in 2002 by both broadcasters.

After the news reports, and reporters had finished with their summing up of mine and my brothers' lives, there was much more to tell, so I decided to tell it as it really was.

It is a life story that is certainly different from most people's lives, and sincerely one I wish I had not experienced. Although I know I will not win any literary awards I hope you will find it interesting, and well told.

I will tell it honestly and to the best of my ability. 'Also adding newspaper cuttings pictures and a Canadian tv video link in the last few pages of the book.

For over twenty years I have lived part of my life in Whiston Merseyside, trying to be that ordinary person, but this news item was bringing me questions enquiring about my past from family, and friends.

I tried my best to explain why the media had covered the story but felt there was so much missing in my answers.

One night as I browsed through some old photographs, I thought to myself when they were taken, they didn't mean too much to whoever had taken them and had been put away in a drawer without a second thought, certainly not knowing they would become such an important and vital link to my story.

I reflected it's only when you look back years later certain photographs become a magical snapshot of your life.

As the night drew on, I sat back, closed my eyes, and wondered about what my neighbours had said, and pondered hard on how I could explain my story through extracts taken from newspapers, and television, these articles which only told a tiny part of my life.

Which I will share with you at the end of my story, giving you an insight into three brothers' lives affected so differently than some of their comments of everything will be alright "new life softens tragedy" reports implied.

With that thought in my mind, I began in earnest putting pen to paper.

Thankfully my brother Michael presented me with evidence of a journey my mother had taken before my birth which was the one missing link in my knowledge of past events, but so needed to complete the whole story.

My name is Robert; Turley I was born on the 14th of February 1950 Saint Valentine's Day in a Victorian hospital called Mill Road in Liverpool.

I have in my mind repeated this location many times just to remind myself I had a mother, which you will come to understand as to why as my story continues.

Not long after my birth On the 15th of March 1950 aged one month and one day, I was taken in my Mother's arms on board the Empress of Canada ship which was docked in Liverpool and about to leave for Montreal in Canada.

Life for me and my two-year-old brother Danny was about to continue a long way from our birthplace in England.

Please bear with me as I now have to take you back in time to events before my birth to establish how my story came about, and as to why I have this sad, yet interesting story to tell.

I will continue with a small account of my mother's and fathers life which without a doubt gives the word fate a huge part in my story, and brings an early sadness to my words.

The account of my mother Victoria and my father Danny's meeting is only brief within my story, just a few pages, but needed to complete the whole story.

My mother Victoria Craddock was born in Montreal on 24th September 1928 to English parents who had settled in Canada.

She had black hair, an olive complexion, and brown eyes. She grew up within a family which could be described as middle class; academically she achieved well and was fluent in French, essential in mainly French-speaking Montreal.

At the age of 14 on completion of her exams, she left school, a young woman with a promising future.

At the time of my account in 1942, Montreal was overflowing with merchant ships from all over the world Many of the ships were from England and docked in Canada taking on supplies to support their people and allies who were at war with Germany.

Sailors weary from months at sea were helped by Canadian churches.

Hostels were set up to bring comfort and rest to the many seamen arriving.

With so many needing food and shelter, Canadian people agreed to help. Victoria and her two sisters worked in one of the hostels for about 3 years

Victoria was 17 yrs. old when the war in Europe ended, the Nazis defeated. People rejoiced, and prayed for a peaceful future.

It was during this period my mother's destiny was to be determined.

Many Sailors who stayed at the hostel where she worked had asked her for a date without success until she met Danny.

Danny, was twenty-one he had joined the Merchant navy from his home port in Liverpool at the start of the war in 1942 when 18 years old.

Merchant seamen were the unsung heroes of the Second World War, young and old served knowing of the danger during this hostile time, their ships being easy targets for German U boats in the battle for control of the Atlantic Ocean.

During those 4 years of war, my father served on nine different merchant ships sailing to various destinations in Europe and North America.

At the beginning of his service, he served as a galley boy, and then as he got older and stronger, he became a fireman stoking the ship's furnaces with coal.

Ex merchant seamen have informed me this job was one of the toughest in the merchant navy, not for the faint-hearted, apart from the hard work a hit from a torpedo below deck meant little chance of survival.

During this period my father's strong character would have been formed, a time when men had to cope under extreme pressure, character, and pressure that would be tested to the full as my story continues.

His ship was docked in Montréal and anchored up for repairs. which gave him extended shore leave and extra time to spend with newly met Victoria.

Quite soon into their relationship Victoria introduced him to her family; unfortunately, this meeting did not go well with my mother's tee-total family, he was unaware the family was teetotal.

His mistake at taking a drink before meeting them meant they took an instant dislike of him, also they felt their daughter could do better than to get involved with a merchant sailor, with their reputation of being here today and gone tomorrow.

Sadly, in less than six months and before their relationship developed or had been accepted, Victoria's father died from a heart attack, she must have been devestated.it was a cruel blow

Also, at this sad time Danny's shore leave expired, the ship's repairs were completed all crew was summoned back to ship, but reporting to ship was the last thing on his mind, Victoria had just buried her dad, he had also fallen in love, this to him was no time to leave, so he decided to jump ship.

As the months passed Victoria discovered she was pregnant. With this news, Danny asked for the needed consent of her mother to marry.

She reluctantly agreed. With this permission, they wasted no time and married on 13th December 1946 in St Aiden's church Montreal.

In such a short period Victoria had fallen in love, lost her father, became pregnant, and married, adding to these life-changing events her mother, and sisters implied the stress her father had felt about her relationship with Danny had hastened his death. Shunned by her family, she and her husband were left to go it alone.

These dramatic events drew them closer together and they looked to the future with optimism.

Canada was a young country where countless opportunities could arise. Unfortunately, their hopes and plans for the future had a huge setback.

The Canadian authorities were pursuing Danny for jumping ship, and because of this, he was classified as an illegal immigrant.

When they caught up with him he pleaded his case, but no sympathy was shown by immigration, even though my father was now married to a Canadian citizen who was carrying his child the authorities would not change their policy, he was ordered to leave on the next ship out of Montreal, and wouldn't be allowed to return for two years.

There would be no free ride out of Canada; he was assigned to a merchant ship the Manchester trader; his punishment was to work onboard for his passage back to England.

Given little time to say goodbye to Victoria he told her to be patient until his return.

The thought of being 3 thousand miles for two years was unbearable. They wanted to share the joy of their first-born child, on leaving Danny passed her his address, 20 Eaton Place Everton Liverpool.

After he had left, she decided her son would be born with both parents present, no rules in her mind were going to stop that happening, with her savings she made plans to make the long journey by ship to England.

Now well into her pregnancy, Victoria prepared herself for the journey ahead. Securing her passage, she sent a telegram saying, Danny "Arriving Southampton July 8th on Aquitania love. Vicky.

On departure day her first sighting of the ship called Aquitania, a huge four-funnelled vessel must have amazed her; the ship she was about to board was equal in size to the Titanic, and had been given the nickname "The Ship Beautiful ".

Aquitania had been used as a hospital ship during the 1st world war, and as a troop carrier during the 2nd world war.

At the time of Victoria's embarkation, the ship was being used as a war brides' carrier.

Whether or not Victoria knew of this great ship's past would have meant little to her, she was now eight months into her pregnancy, and worried about departing to a destination of which she knew very little, but there was no turning back, she had made her decision.

Of the many people on board who received loving hugs and waves goodbye, sadly she left without any fond farewells from her stubborn family.

The journey across the Atlantic on this huge ship Aquitania would have been a unique experience for Victoria.

Arriving in Southampton after the long 3000-mile Atlantic crossing, then the subsequent 250-mile train journey to Liverpool heavily pregnant, Victoria finally arrived in her husband's city.

Hard Times

Her first observations arriving in Liverpool must have been daunting, during the war the city had been severely bombed leaving the landscape scarred with buildings blackened by smoke and fire, so unlike her native Canada which had been left unscathed by warfare.

Liverpool was so different from her native city of Montreal, the Everton area was densely populated with back to back terraced housing, it must have felt so enclosed with all the houses so close to each other, looking identical row after row street after street, very different to the wide-open spaces of Montreal.

Most streets in the area where my mother was about to reside would have had large gaps in between houses , homes which had been blown to bits by German bombs.

Liverpool was one of the British cities most targeted by the German bombers due to its docks being the main supply line to the North Atlantic, and Everton being just one and a half miles from the docks had taken a lot of damage.

Rationing was in place and had been since the start of the 2nd world war 5 yrs. earlier. Also, Britain was just getting over a bitterly cold winter; she would have noticed the long queues at various shops in the area where basics like bread and potatoes were hard to find.

She would also have observed the poor state of the children in the area dressed in shabby clothes, worn-out shoes playing in the dangerous buildings left partially standing, remnants of German air raids.

Noticeably on most street corners, there was a public house selling beer with some of these children's parents within, and oblivious to what their children were up to whilst drinking cheap intoxicating local ale.

To a young 18-year-old Canadian woman these observations would have been a total culture shock.

On arrival at my father's home, she would have been dismayed, it was a hovel poorly lit by gas with no electricity connected.

The house built in Victorian times had no bathroom with a single structured outside toilet.

The property was rented by my father's parents and a disgrace to the landlord.

A dwelling crowded with three generations of one family.

Although almost certainly worried by the conditions she encountered she was with her husband, and both soon to become parents.

Joyfully thirty-seven days after arriving in England on 14th August 1947, she gave birth to a boy

He was named Daniel George, Daniel after her husband, and George in memory of her father, names agreed on by my parents with care showing respect for one another in their choice.

Living in such poor conditions with a baby to care for would become an uphill struggle. On cold windy days, poorly fitted doors and windows offered little protection against the elements.

To meet the challenge of keeping their baby sheltered, and well would take total commitment.

England's housing had been described by a Member of Parliament Bessie Braddock in these words: "Our people are living in flea-ridden, bug-ridden rat-ridden hellholes"., A lot of dwellings in the Everton area fell into this category.

Crippled by the expense of war it seemed it would stay that way for some time giving a bleak outlook all over England for many years to come.

For a lot of men and women, the poverty was made worse by the constant draw of the alehouse, it was for many the only escape from the reality they faced each day.

This resulted in the neglect of their homes, their children, and themselves.

To improve their family's lives, finding any type of work for many men was a lottery, such a distressing time.

My mother had never before encountered anything like this poor way of life unlike many of the women around her who were perhaps more accustomed, although similarly distressed by their circumstances.

She would have hoped for a speedy return to Canada.

Sixteen months later November 18, 1948, my mother gave birth to her second child and named him Victor Alexander, this being the boy's version of my mother's name, as with their first child agreed by both of my parents.

Victor sadly was not a strong baby the freezing winter, and damp living conditions took their toll, he lived for thirty-eight days dying on Christmas Eve 1948.

On his death certificate, the cause of death was given as marasmus, an illness many babies died from throughout Britain, during these really hard times.

To lose Victor on Christmas Eve normally a day of joy even in the toughest of times would have left my parents with an empty hollow feeling so hard to take.

My parents had suffered the cruellest of blows: the death of a child, a tiny 6-pound baby born to be loved but cruelly taken away.

Now and always the eve before Christmas would be a painful memory of Victor.

How they coped in the times ahead must have been extremely distressing, almost unimaginable.

Losing a partner, you are a widow, losing parents' an orphan, but no words describe the death of a child.

Managing their grief there was still their toddler Danny to care for and as time passed during natural husband and wife relations fourteen months later on February 14th, 1950 I Robert was born.

At the time of my birth my mother had been in England for two years and six months. She had experienced the joy of her first son, and suffered the pain of losing a child.

She had given birth three times in less than three years while living in poor conditions and uncertain of the future.

With no signs of improvement in her situation, as a mother she must have felt very concerned for her two small son's welfare, she was still young herself, just 21 years old living thousands of miles from home, and surely missing her family.

In hope for a speedy return to Canada my mother penned a letter to her mother outlining her desperation.

Although my father's pride would be denied, he would have realised his wife was now a protective mother, he would have known he couldn't raise the funds on the wages which prevailed, like it or not he would have to agree to her asking for help. That help was given by her mother in the form of shipping tickets (costing £54 10d per adult) I've been informed children less than 3 years old went free, the tickets purchased were to assist her daughter and children with no consideration for my father her dislike of him had not changed from their first meeting.

In her opinion the longer her daughter was away from my father the better as she felt babies were being produced too often.

Liverpool to Montreal

ON the 15th of March 1950 aged one month I was taken by my mother along with my 3-year-old brother on board the Empress of Canada ship which was about to leave Liverpool for Montreal in Canada.

Aged twenty-one my mother was leaving Liverpool without any intention of returning, and wondering when she would see her husband again, but foremost in her mind would have been her children's future.

During the 3000-mile Atlantic crossing from Liverpool, to Pier 21 Halifax Nova Scotia, she was not in the best of health. Thankfully she found herself in the company of a young Irish couple travelling to Canada, they kindly assisted my mother from time to time with her babies, my brother and I.

On her arrival in Canada, she set up home in a small house on the south shore of Montreal, at 3276 Grand Boulevard.

This area on the south shore of Montreal was known as Mackayville. Back in her home city, she was happy in the place she loved and important to her bringing up her sons as Canadians.

As we settled into our new surroundings, she felt secure and more at peace. It had not been long since my birth, and as her health improved, she would have felt proud in achieving a better life for her family, and yet sometimes sad at what she had been through.

My mother corresponded with my father hoping for any news of his return.

Eventually, he found a merchant ship and worked on his passage to Canada.

In the coming months, he obtained Canadian citizenship and found employment as a crane driver for a steel company.

Continuing in regular employment he was able to purchase decent items to make a more comfortable home

Now a much-improved life was being achieved far away from England, and its poverty.

How proud my parents must have felt to now feed and dress their family well. Returning to Montreal was proving her decision was right.

During these happier times two more children were born, Michael on 22nd March 1953, and Russell on the 6th January 1955.

The family now extended to four boys, overcrowded the house on Grand Boulevard became a little small, still in the same area of Mackayville, now known as La Fleche, a larger house was found, 1525 De Gaulle Street, a rented single-story house owned by a Frenchman, whose name was Mr. Vincent.

Encouraging anyone with spare land Montreal had a policy during the early 1950s to build much-needed housing with whatever materials were available.

This particular house was built of wood with a tar paper roof, well-insulated from the severe Canadian winters, and quite normal for Montreal at the time.

Everything was going well, a new house, a car, and the news of a new addition to our family. My mother had her sixth child Kevin on 2nd July 1957.

How times change seven years earlier my mother left Liverpool with the sad loss of her baby, she now had five sons.

Relevant in telling my story I must go through the few memories I had during my childhood years in Canada, not that amazing or much different than any child's life, but to me, as my life was to pan out so important to cherish, and keep in my memory.

My earliest memories of growing up in Montreal are from the age of four.

Added to these vivid memories by years of research, are pictures of my family, pictures, and documentation I never knew existed until much later in life

Some of the memories are of being part of a family being loved, and cared for, with parents who guide, and reassure whenever needed.

I have lovely memories of bursting with pride when aged around six years old walking up and down the road like a soldier on parade, dressed smartly in a brown shirt, matching trousers, and shoes, it was a wonderful moment in time.

Although I was young in years, I sensed the feeling known as brotherly love. Especially was the love I felt for toddler Russell with his cheeky grin and chubby legs, sensing without being told it would always be my duty to watch over all my brothers, feelings that have never left me.

I was without a doubt at the beginning of understanding the importance of becoming part of a family unit which meant pulling together as one.

For example, there was the time my brother Danny slashed his leg in the soft tissue directly behind his kneecap, at the back of his leg.

I noticed it whilst walking behind him.

The gash was about two inches across with strangely no blood showing. He was unaware of his wound until I pointed it out. He then started to panic.

My mother very quickly calmed him and expertly stitched his wound herself.

We were amazed at her skill and comforted in what a wonderful mother we had.

She was always there to comfort us like when for no one apparent reason I or my brothers woke in the middle of the night, and sat next to her feeling warm Cosy, watching TV, and waiting for my father to return from his late shift.

One evening dad turned up driving a big dark blue American style car. We were so excited.

The car had a bulbous shape to it; I can't remember the make but loved the silver badge on the bonnet.

Then there was the smell of leather from the seats, although not new still giving off that unmistakable smell.

All the family was pleased.

I recall a song, ``Stranger in Paradise". By the Four Aces, I especially remember the wonderful voices of the people who sang that beautiful song, their voices echoed all through our house.

Small things like this, with Mum singing along to the radio whilst making bread.

My special memories of a happy home. Outside home I had to face life's ups and downs

Like at school on my way out of class I took some discarded paper from a scrap bin, I was seen by a teacher told off, then hit with a leather strap across my hand.

I still feel the sting in my fingers to this day.

Taking the paper from a waste bin was classed as stealing.

I didn't think I was treated fairly, but not knowing much about right or wrong at five years old I took the punishment, and never told my parents.

It was my first harsh lesson at the beginning of my life's journey.

Then there was the scary time one summer's day in a field near our home.

Dad got involved in an argument with several neighbours who he had been drinking with.

I remember as it got nasty watching in amazement as the men came towards him, dad whipped his belt from his trouser loops, and wrapped it around his fist if they wished to fight, he was ready I was petrified; thankfully my mother appeared and spoke a few harsh words to all concerned ending the incident peacefully.

Like a lot of family's, we had a pet dog, a St Bernard named Smokey.

He was huge I could sit on playfully not causing him any discomfort.

I remember it was a sad time when he died due to something he had eaten.

Dad buried Smokey in our backyard. We marked the spot with a wooden cross.

Happily, there were many good memories, like playing with my brothers Danny and Michael on our sleds in the deep snows of winter.

Sometimes it snowed so hard Dad would have to shovel four feet of snow away from our front door, how he got out of the door in the first place with all the snow blocking it I never knew, on those days' dad was our hero.

I remember a short ten-mile journey to an Indian reservation called Caughnawaga, home of the Iroquois Indians.

Billy Two Rivers, a well-known wrestler from the 1950s became a well-respected representative for the people on this reservation.

After the visit, influenced by where we had been my brothers, and I dressed in our cowboy suits, and played cowboy Indian games for many days afterward, looking back it was one of many memorable days out.

Also close to our home was the famous Montreal Canadians Ice Hockey stadium. The Montreal Canadians are 24 times winners of the Stanley Cup.

One of the hockey player's names was Maurice Rocket Richard. In Canada, he was equivalent in stature to the famous footballer George Best of Britain.

When I watched TV or listened to the radio, Rocket's name would always pop up. With the influence of ice hockey, the Maple leaf flag of Canada at school, and my mother's teachings, I was becoming a full-blown Canadian.

In July 1957 my brother Kevin was born, he brought joy to our family, especially on the day of his christening.

By December that year, ten years had passed since my mother's marriage, six boys had been born. She was now 29 years old, her wedding anniversary was approaching bringing memories that would surely have taken her back to her son Victor who had died nine years earlier in that same month.

She would not have dwelt long on these thoughts with five children to care for; she would have soon been back to her routine, cooking, washing, and ironing, and yet still finding time for eagerly awaited bedtime stories.

Mother always made time for stories, intermingled with French pronunciations aiding in our education, preparing us for life in bilingual Montreal.

Being December, my brothers and I focused all our thoughts on the excitement of Christmas, as we believed Santa would soon be visiting.

The Shops in Montreal encouraged these feelings, their windows crammed with presents depicting the magic of Christmas. All was well with my family.

On 2nd December a bitterly cold 16-degrees-below zero night- we had all gone to bed after a meal of spaghetti Bolognese with Boston cream pie, a meal remembered by Danny. All tucked up warm and cosy when BANG! – The door to mine and my brother's bedroom flew open.

With eyes half open, unable to see in the dark we were dragged out of bed terrified with no clue as to why this was happening, dad seemed in a rage grabbing at us shouting, and banging on the wall with his fists "What had we done?" was the thought that went through my mind, too startled and rushed to even begin to shed a tear we were thrown into the street, shivering with cold and fear then watched my father rush back to the house.

Still not fully aware of what was happening seeing him open our front door and being forced back by huge flames bursting towards his face.

Now fully awake our nightmare had begun.

As we stood their trembling neighbours came to our aid, wrapped us in blankets and carried us away from the raging fire.

A neighbour, Mr. Brunel gave us shelter. I remember looking back in disbelief at the huge fire against the black sky, sensing the smell, and hearing screaming voices from all directions, added to by loud crackling sounds from the flames engulfing the property from within.

My home where we had been so happy was now burning savagely.

Through the mayhem, my most frightening memory was hearing frantic shouting from people crying out my mother's, and brother's names.

Once the fire had taken hold the flames moved through the property with relentless speed, 3 Fire appliances arrived 15 minutes after frantic calls were made, but were not prepared for what they encountered, the ferocity, and speed of the fire were overwhelming for these seasoned fire-fighters.

The blaze had claimed three lives.

I was two months from my eighth birthday and could not fully contemplate what dire straits my family now had to face. I knew what was happening was horrendous, and such was the horror of that frightening night, I instinctively knew it would always haunt me.

One thought that went through my head that night was how mine and my family's life had changed forever, I was fully awake living a nightmare too young to fully understand in what form it would take and when it would end.

Exhausted, squeezing into a tight ball screaming silently, "please this can't be happening" with a sigh so deep I felt like my ribs would collapse, distraught I fell asleep.

That morning on the 3rd of December 1957 the press put their versions of events: French and English newspapers wrote of my mother's bravery in great detail, of a mother returning into a burning building trying to save her sons.

She died with Russell in her arms. Kevin in his pushchair all three by the back door so close to escaping. In what seemed like minutes after the fire the press took and printed pictures of our haunted petrified faces, eyes wide open staring back at their cameras.

In one picture no words are needed, they had captured in our expressions the rawness of fear, a fear that no dictionary words could ever compete with.

Life without a mother.

Life now would always be uphill, and for a broken father, hands burnt raw the test was on to find that strong character built from years in dangerous seas.

At that moment we were left still not knowing the full extent of what was unfolding, and the stress we surely were going to face.

The press documented how the intense heat during our rescue had singed our hair. They also printed pictures of shocked firefighters near the smouldering building, seen amongst newspaper articles a large canvas being placed over the remains of my mother, and brothers.

On the 3rd of December just before dawn, my mother woke first. Her cry to my father was: "GET THE CHILDREN OUT – THE HOUSE IS ON FIRE!" Seeing where the fire was at its worst, he made his way to where I and my brothers slept, at the same time shouting to her to get out from the back of the house.

Taking baby Kevin from his cot near to where she slept, she quickly made it to the back door and safety, only to bravely re-enter on hearing the cries of her son Russell but in doing so, was sadly overcome by heat and smoke.

As mentioned earlier my father had rescued my brothers and I. We were safely away from the burning property. My father had tried and tried to re-enter not knowing if his wife or other children were safe, he had been driven back by the intense heat. Neighbours told how he sank to his knees and cried, "Look at that, look at that".

One disturbing article written in the Montreal Gazette newspaper was headed: "MOTHER, TWO SONS TRAPPED IN-HOME, NOT ENOUGH HOSE".

It went on to say the cause of the fire was not known but Mackayville Police and Fire Chief Lucien La Marche told the Gazette on arriving at the burning Turley home 1525 De Gaulle St, he and his men tried to make a connection with the nearest fire hydrant only to find they had an insufficient length of hose. "The nearest hydrant three-quarters of a mile away".

Chief La Marche said "Mr. Turley who was there with his three children told us that his wife 29-year-old Victoria Turley and two children were still in the building.

He said his men fought the blaze with a 1200-gallon capacity tank truck which ran out of water twice and had to be refilled from the nearby hydrant, each trip taking ten to fifteen minutes.

"Three water trucks arrived just after 5.30 am from Croydon and Jacques Cartier and thanks to these we managed to check the blaze before it reached adjoining houses," the chief said. "Thank God the other water trucks arrived in time or half the street might have burnt down. Said Town Councillor Jerry Chiasson, "People blame the mayor and the aldermen but it's not our fault – we don't have the necessary equipment." John Amyot, the chief waterworks engineer in charge of fire protection Canadian underwriters' association, said that "85 percent of Mackayville and all of the parish of St Hubert are classed as without fire protection because their fire-fighting facilities are to all intents non-existent," and city fire director Raymond Pare said that "many municipalities are under-equipped and undermanned, the responsibility rests with each fire chief." Commenting on the Sherbrooke and Mackayville fires and the danger of more fire now that winter was here, he said "People should assure themselves of an escape exit even if there is no apparent possibility of fire; many lives are lost in fires because victims are trapped.

It seems from this newspaper article that while people were losing their lives, a lot of officials were passing the buck.

The truth was there was not enough fire protection.

Never has the cause of the fire been known, unlike today's investigations in times gone by it was more guesswork and very difficult, especially in this case as the house was burnt to its foundations.

Many houses had small electric heaters under their sinks in the hope of keeping the waste and water pipes from freezing.

The only possible reason to be determined was that due to the extreme cold that night the motor jammed, and caused a spark resulting in devastation.

Directly after the fire the hurt my father must have felt is almost indescribable.

Being part of that night and told my mother and brothers were dead I felt so empty.

I along with my Father and brothers all so frightened, and overwhelmed had truly become and would go on as Wounded Souls.

On top of our immediate sorrows at this dreadful time, we received no support from my mother's family.

Unfortunately, my grandmother's grudge remained with my father and it was now going to affect our futures.

In the days ahead, my father had turned to drink, he had lost his wife, his best friend. He must have felt demoralised.

This hard man who had served right through the Second World War was brought to his knees; his hurt so intense that it must have run over and over in his mind that he had not saved half his family.

He now would have to come to terms with his loss and care for his three sons. Soon after the fire The Red Cross organised clothes and collected money donated from the neighbourhood.

Apart from one occasion and traumatised by the recent events the four months from December to April seem almost a complete blank. Only one thing my brother Danny and I recall is a woman named José, who for a short period watched over us.

One day during our stay with this person we were visited by a friend of our family who was shocked to find we were all sobbing when asked why we answered, “She is locking us in the cupboard.”

My father on hearing what the minder had done revealed a side of him we had never encountered before, entering the minder’s house without one word said in a flash the woman was picked up and thrown straight through a set of French doors.

We now knew my dad was not to be messed with.

Shocked at what we had witnessed now whenever in Dad's Company fear of him would affect all three of us from that moment and later in life.

Sweet Jesus as I write of this woman José, I can’t believe what she did, her cruel actions rushed dad to make decisions, not in our best interest and broke further an already shattered family.

Immediately I realised no one was going to care for us like our mother.

Unknown fully whilst so young this was to become a painful reality as our lives moved on.

Due to his distress dad's work was put on hold, he was drinking heavily in a vain attempt to blank out reality.

Pressure grew on him as to what to do with us. In desperation, my father turned for help from our grandmother who told him she would not be able to cope with three young boys, and the best she could suggest was that he put us in boarding school. Not what he wanted to hear, now without the help he had hoped for, decisions were made that added distress to my brothers and myself, everything we had become accustomed to was about to become a distant memory.

My father approached a local reverend who held money collected by the community to aid our future and asked for the money.

With some concern, the reverend asked, "Why do you want the money?" He replied "to send the lads to England" my father explained his in-laws in Montreal offered little help and he was not coping; he had decided it would be best for his sons to be with his relatives in England.

On this request, the reverend arranged a flight for my brothers and I. No arrangements were made for my father to travel at this time, he was to join us sometime in the future.

Explained to the airline by the reverend of our predicament, the airline, with the consent of our father, allowed us to fly without a guardian.

Leaving Canada

It was 4 months after the fire in April of that year, and yet there was still some interest in our lives from the newspapers.

On the day we left the press took pictures of the three of us saying goodbye to father, press flashbulbs going pop one of the few memories remembered by five-year-old Michael during that sad departure day.

Looking back at the press photographs anyone without previous knowledge of events may take it we were about to embark on a holiday, this was a far cry from the truth which I will more than touch on, and reveal as my story continues.

The media took several more photographs and then in a flash Dad was gone. Alone petrified boarding the aeroplane not knowing our destination or fate, worrying, and not quite understanding why dad was not travelling with us, we took our seats.

The aeroplane we were to travel on was a propeller-type owned by TransCanada Airlines.

Once onboard, we had tags with our names attached to our coats to assist the stewardesses in identifying us during our flight.

We were treated kindly on the aeroplane and given replicas of the aircraft.

During our flight, I remember my ears hurting, being frightened, and wondering what lay ahead at the end of our journey.

The flight and length of time it had taken to arrive in England left our emotions at an all-time low.

Arriving in England.

We arrived at Heathrow airport on the 23rd of April, 1958, on Saint George's Day.

The Canadian press had passed our story on to the newspapers and TV in England.

As a result, we were filmed by BBC News as we walked down the steps of the aircraft.

It was a short film commentated on by Kenneth Kendal a famous BBC newsreader who was at the beginning of his career.

At London's Heathrow airport we were met by my father's step-sister Eva who had relatives in the capital.

The press took pictures, with headlines "Orphans fly home to a new life with relatives" and "new life softens tragedy".

Yes, we felt orphaned, the headline a new life softens tragedy was somewhat premature, we were fretting for our mother, yet no one seemed to Understand.

Our first few days in England were spent in London's East End, a place known as Mile End.

After a short stay, we boarded a train at Euston for our journey to Liverpool. Arriving in the city we were now in a different neighbourhood, nothing like the open spaces known to us in Canada.

In Liverpool the continuous rows of terraced houses and smoking chimneys were the only things you could see in any direction, cobbled streets dominated the area, there didn't seem to be a tree or a blade of grass in view, it seemed so grey and gloomy, perhaps also the fog I was experiencing for the first time gave that impression to the surroundings.

Street lamps spaced out along the cobbled streets gave an illuminated glow as night time approached.

The housing situation in the Everton area had not progressed or improved; it still had similar surroundings encountered by my mother ten years earlier in 1947.
Poverty was still an issue, for her husband to send her sons to the place she had left behind 8 years earlier to give them a better future, words quoted of turning in your grave would certainly question the decision he had made.

Split amongst relatives

We were taken to Eaton Place, the property my mother had left behind eight years earlier. We were guided into the main room at the front of the house, there stood a group of people not known to my brothers or me, then one of the adults spoke out, "who do you want to go with?" My five-year-old brother Michael was petrified there was no way he could have understood what was happening.
Straightaway Eva said: "I will take him." Michael was picked up and gone in a flash, Danny and I glanced at each other with a worried look. We were left with the feeling of not knowing when we would see him again. "Who do you want to go with"?" I was asked.
I was very upset and confused, as I looked around, I noticed one woman who had a look of my father, I pointed to this lady "OK, you will be staying with Aunt Liz.", my brother Danny was told "You will be staying here with your gran", and Aunt Mary". It was then we were told not to worry, "we are your father's family" I didn't feel comforted by these words, I felt alone, separated from my brothers, and uncertain of times ahead.
I was taken by my father's sister Aunt Liz to her home, a three-bedroomed terraced house still in the Everton district of Liverpool – the address was 25 Copeland Street.
The house was heated by a coal fire, the inside of the property consisted of a front, and a back room with a small kitchen to the rear, at the back of the property there was a small backyard with an outside toilet.
These properties when built were not designed to incorporate inside bathrooms.
A tin bath filled manually from buckets was the only way of washing.
The walls were painted in a yellow distemper; I was warned not to rub against this chalky substance as it stained your clothes.

As I entered the house for the first time a young lad was washing in a white butler sink located in the kitchen, my back turned without any warning I was hit on the back of the head with a large block of soap thrown by this boy, perhaps it was a jealous act as I was the centre of attention on the day.

This was my introduction to my cousin Stan. It may have seemed amusing to Stan at the time, but was not for me.

Stan proved to be a mischievous character. He would not have presumed his actions were malicious in any way, he just thought it was a laugh, but for me being separated from my brothers in a strange house with family I did not yet know it was far from funny.

I felt so alone that first night.

My aunt Liz was married to George. They had five kids. Danny, their eldest son, was serving in the British Army, the King's Regiment.

He boxed, and played football for his regiment, and was fortunate to play a friendly game against the England World cup team Just before the 1966 tournament started.

Jean, their eldest daughter, was married.

Words are not easy to describe her.

She was the kindest person I've ever met.

She would always ask me how I felt.

Jean told me of her childhood memories when in my mother's company; she said she adored my mother.

When she spoke, I felt so proud of hearing her words and of the impression my mother had left on her.

She mentioned many times that my mother had promised her the chance to experience life in Canada, a promise that sadly now could never happen.

Their second daughter Doreen was a very pretty girl, often when her mum and dad were out, she would have her girlfriends, and sometimes boys in the house.

One night, as I sat watching them fool around, one of the boys wearing Cuban heel boots, stood on my toe! It left me in agony; when he examined his boot, he discovered why I was in so much pain, a large nail was sticking out of the heel.

After that, I made myself scarce when Doreen had her friends' round.

Betty, the youngest daughter, was born within a year of my arrival at my aunt's. I watched over her like an angel, whenever I was near her, she would always be in my arms preferring no one else, and I loved looking after her.

In my aunt's house, the sleeping arrangements were tight; I shared a bed with my newfound cousin Stan.

The bedroom furniture was sparse, just a bed, and an old wardrobe, the bed covering was limited, to keep us warm old coats, and coarse army blankets were used.

Stan had the unfortunate problem of bedwetting making the centre of the bed a no-go area, apart from when you would unknowingly turn over in your sleep towards the centre of the bed.

Danny, my eldest brother, was being watched over by my father's sister Mary, her husband Sid, along with their son Michael, and our grandparents.

All I remember of my grandmother was that she was called Ninny, Ninny being a local name for grandmothers in the area.

My grandfather was a First World War veteran; he suffered the loss of one eye during this period. He was a grumpy man who always sat by his coal fire shouting for quiet when noise levels were raised.

In the two years before being taken to Canada in 1950 my grandmother had bonded with my brother Danny.

Now unexpectedly she had a second chance to make a fuss of him. She cared for him like a son until her death, within a year of his return.

Her death was an added blow to Danny, the loss of another close family member so soon after the death of our mother.

My brother Danny had it tough in Eaton Place; it couldn't be any other way. Conditions had not changed in the ten years of my mother's experience.

Now at school mixing with other children who were living in similar conditions, he was constantly infested with hair lice.

Hair lice were rife, and passed on to all within close contact, untreated the problem did not improve.

Aunty Mary, like many local people, had not received the best education; although poor she was a kind person.

Mary had suffered a brain tumour operation some years earlier; this limited her capabilities making the day-to-day life struggle harder.

Danny on many occasions was left to fend for himself; Danny recalled that within days of arriving at Eaton place the clothes he had brought from Canada went missing.

He soon learned it was a case of first-up, best dressed at Eaton Place.

I have heard it said when you live in poverty and have not experienced anything else it could be perceived as normal, perhaps it's true, but for me and Danny life was so different, we had experienced a loving home life with a mother, and father caring for us, life in Liverpool at that time was the complete opposite in that it would take time to adjust to our family relations, although loving, not our parents.

The hope we carried was to be reunited together on our father's return to England.

My late mother's sister Violet had married an Englishman named Dennis and had moved to England from Canada, and now lived in Birmingham.

On a visit to Liverpool to see her three nephews she first called on Michael. She found him in a sorry state, terribly thin, and covered in scabs; Eva explained to the aunt that he would only eat small amounts of cereals.

Violet recognized Michael was not well and at risk, she told Eva she was taking custody of her nephew, and he would be returning to Birmingham with her.

Eva maybe relieved did not object. Once home in Birmingham she called on her doctor after an examination the doctor told aunt violet that Michael was suffering from malnutrition, poor appetite, and lack of nourishment, the likely cause was the trauma of losing his mother and being separated from his two brothers would also have impacted on him.

The doctor advised Michael's health would improve.

During his four years living in Birmingham with aunty Volet and Uncle Dennis Michael shared a good family life, he enjoyed summer holidays in the south of England, with this care and attention he blossomed into a well-educated eight-year-old.

Violet and Dennis had a son named David; he was twelve months older than my brother Michael.

They were happy, contented boys well looked after and loved.

Only once in four years during my stay with Aunt Liz did I get to be with my brothers, it was one summer's day in 1959. In a surprise visit my Aunt Violet turned up in Liverpool with Michael, we were all taken on a day out to the seaside a place called New Brighton.

Just being together for that one day at the seaside was fantastic. Three brothers reunited wow.

We had a picnic and were treated to ice cream, and candy floss which made the day even more special.

It was a wonderful gesture by an aunt, and will always be a cherished childhood memory. Later I was dropped off at my Aunt Liz's house.

I hugged and squeezed my brother's goodbye, and was tearful as they were driven away. I felt crushed after being so happy all day, and now so sad seeing them leave.

My day was slightly spoiled when Aunt Liz complained my cousin Stan had been left behind and thought it unfair.

In Violet's defence, she made this trip for separated brothers to be together, there was no malice, or intention to offend my aunt or uncle in any way, Aunt Liz's comment was upsetting, she just didn't see the bigger picture, or understand what it meant to us.

For once in my life, I felt no guilt, nothing could take away that special day. The next day it was back to a normal routine no further comments were made, I think my aunt had realised after some thought, no harm was done.

My aunt and uncle struggled to make ends meet.

My uncle was a labourer on various building sites during the sixties when it rained, or if the company saw fit, he was laid off without pay.

This sadly was often the case.

He was a good honest man who loved to bake, his specialty being Madeira cake.

My father's mother, and both sisters Mary, and Liz worked all the entrances into Anfield cemetery from the early 1900s, selling flowers to the bereaved.

Control of these entrances was no easy feat, in Liverpool.

Every Sunday morning hail rain or shine my Aunt Liz would set up her flowers outside the main gate of the cemetery. earning a profit from her flowers would depend on the weather when it rained sales were poor, which would mean a harder week ahead.

During my three years living with my aunt, and uncle I would run every errand requested of me as I felt obliged to do so.

Life was tough for them, now in me, they had another person to feed, and clothe. They were kind people who enjoyed a drink to escape the hard-living conditions. When I arrived on their doorstep expenditure was already fully stretched.

Apart from Cousin Jean, my past was rarely mentioned during my years with Aunt Liz. The only time any mentions of events in Canada were made was when I was introduced to people as Danny's son who lost his mother in a fire. "Poor lad," people would say, it was at these times that I would bow my head, and feel saddened at being reminded my mother was lost, holding in my emotions, but inwardly feeling the hurt of missing my family, and reliving that tragic night.

My brothers and I could have done with any kind of counselling, but none was offered there was no awareness of how as an eight-year-old I felt.

Throughout the years I dealt with my grief alone, as it is true children in the 50s and 1960s were seen, but not heard.

Football or what you may call soccer was unknown to me in Canada. Their national sport was Ice hockey.

Now in England, I was introduced to football which I enjoyed. I Spent most days outside kicking a ball with local boys.

All my sorrow disappeared during those games. The ideal place to play was at the back of Aunt Liz's house where there was a large alleyway; Heyworth Street Infants School which I attended was on the opposite adjoining side of the alleyway.

Whenever the school caretaker saw me having heard my Canadian accent he would start singing "The Wild Canadian boy, the Wild Canadian boy" over and over again. I don't know if there ever was such a song with that title or that he had just made it up himself, but it was quite amusing, and always made me smile.

When at school I could not wait for playtime so I could be back kicking a ball, playing football took my mind off my worries; it took me to another place away from all the stress I felt. It was in that alleyway where I developed my dribbling skills playing against local kids, my cousin, Stan, although a menace became a lovable friend when he started to join in the games of football.

Close to Four years had passed in 1961 when I was told my father was, at last, coming back to England, this to me was wonderful news, he was our hero our dad. News of his return meant at last my brothers and I would be together ending our separate lives, to be back as a family meant so much.

On his arrival back in England, dad moved into Eaton Place. There was never any explanation given to myself or my brothers as to why it took him four years to join us. Just having him back in our lives was more important than that time.

The four years apart from dad and what he did in Canada remain a mystery and never spoken about. Most days on his return to Eaton place my father was out and about trying to find somewhere for us all to live.

When in our company on other days we had to compete with relatives who could not get him to the pub quickly enough.

On his return to England my father seemed to have plenty of money and nice clothes, also apparent in his generosity, like when someone commented on his nice Canadian leather jacket, he immediately took it off and gave it to his admirer, my dad making it obvious to me he had no interest in material things.

When under the influence of drink, a nasty side of my father would erupt. After visiting the pub back at Auntie's house some words would be exchanged with one of my uncles and all hell would be let loose.

I observed my father could be one of the scariest men you would ever want to meet, especially when he lost his temper, a temper which seemed to be always on a short fuse making everybody careful of what they said when in his company.

I was still living with Aunt Liz but would visit him whenever I could, in the hope to be told we'd soon be all together, during my visits I got to play with Danny and the kids who lived in his area.

On one of those days, my father joined in a game of cricket, as did a few other adults. One of these adults was a woman called May.

Life with May.

As a child at the time, I can only describe her as looking very similar to Hilda Ogden the character from the TV soap Coronation Street, like the character Hilda she always had rollers in her hair.

She was a married woman with two children and lived in a terrace house opposite 20 Eaton Place. Father very quickly struck up what was perceived by me as a friendly relationship with her.

Every time I visited my father May would be sure to appear and say hello, nine times out of ten bringing sweets or chocolate.

On one occasion she was extremely nice towards me, giving me a whole one-pound note, and saying here you go son run, and bye yourself some sweets, and by the way you can keep the change.

Wow, a pound that was a lot of money for a child in 1961, she had me hooked.

At that moment in time, I thought she was wonderful, she seemed so caring.

My father is now 37 yrs.' old, arriving back in England 4 yrs.' After the death my mother left him vulnerable to any female attention, and likewise for me as a child with no mother her being so extremely kind, gave me hope life was changing for the better.

She seemed to become besotted with my father very quickly into their relationship. She left her husband and two children, a boy and a girl, I never met her children and there was never any talk of them joining up to become part of an extended family, which even as a child I wondered as to why.

At the beginning of my father's and May's relationship, I was once taken by them both to the cinema to see the first showing of the James Bond film, Dr. No.

After watching the film walking home my father told me he had found a place for us to live, two rooms in Queen's Road, Everton.

He went on to tell me he was going to bring Michael home from Birmingham, and that May was going to live, and care for us.

One thing my father made clear to me was that there would only ever be one woman he truly loved, he also said he would never remarry, this comment from my father was the one, and only time he ever spoke to me of my mother.

I was so happy my young brother was coming back after such a long time apart.

The only problem was with my brother Danny he was not happy with May coming into our life.

Danny told me he knew of May from his experience of living in Eaton Place, and that she was known to have a reputation of flirting with workmen from the Double Diamond beer works situated at the bottom of Eaton Place, many others in the area held the same view of her.

Early into their relationship my father, May, Danny, and I moved as promised into Queen's Road. I can only describe the house in Queen's road as a dump; the rooms had holes in the ceilings from years of neglect.

One room which was to be our bedroom had old TVs, and radios stored in it, they were not taken away just shoved aside to make room for a bed.

Given to us by the Salvation Army was a bed, and mattress, these items were not in the best of condition hygienically speaking, but at that moment in time, the saying beggars can't be choosers springs to mind.

In the house there was a cooker on one of the landings, which was shared by two other families, with one toilet to be shared by all who lived in the house, there was no bathroom.

The front door was always on the latch, or perhaps broken, the room my brothers and I stayed in had no lock, thinking back I realise this was not a safe environment for young boys to sleep in.

It must have been a hasty decision by my father, and May to accept this extremely poor accommodation.

I can only suspect getting away from her husband was the reason why it was taken with such haste.

As promised my father went to Violet's in Birmingham to bring Michael back to where we all felt he belonged.

Danny and I had not seen our little brother for over three years.

We couldn't sleep or think of anything else knowing he was coming back.

The day dad picked him up, aunt Violet Uncle Dennis, his school friends, and teachers were broken-hearted that he was about to leave. Violet and Dennis tried to persuade my father to let him stay but their pleas fell on deaf ears, dad was bringing us all together.

In anticipation of Michaels' return all that day Danny, and I watched from our bedroom window at the top of the three-story dump in Queen's Road waiting for his arrival.

When at last we spotted Michael we nearly broke our necks running downstairs to get to him.

Over three years, and now together again I can only describe it as heavenly.

That day an unbelievable bond wrapped itself around the three of us.

The first few hours with Michael were fantastic listening to his Birmingham accent.

We could tell he had been well looked after by the smart way he had been dressed.

As we settled down from out of his suitcase Michael presented his brothers with some comics, and cakes neatly wrapped by Auntie.

Then he produced a gift better than all the cakes, comics, and money in the world, three photographs, one of our Mother, and two pictures of us all together as a family in Canada.

Pictures that showed a happy past, we couldn't stop staring at them.

One of the photographs was our mother, and of our two lost brothers they were no longer just a memory, we had their images.

Wonderful pictures of 5 children smartly dressed creases in our trousers hair well-groomed standing shoulder to shoulder in a straight line with our Mother looking so proud [. As seen on the cover of my book].

There was also a picture of us dressed up in our cowboy suits, which I have remembered vividly over the years.

The pictures showed us smiling, looking happy, and content.

These wonderful pictures were now imprinted in our minds; thanks to my mother's sister these pictures would at least give us a focus for the rest of our lives to try to recreate those magical moments in time.

Excitedly we approached our father with the photographs, but he refused to look at them saying "It's all in here" as he pointed to his head, "I don't need pictures." We turned away from him, heads bowed deflated by his words, as young boys not understanding his reasons but left feeling like we had just lost our mother, and brothers all over again, and at the same time knowing we must not speak of the pictures or mother with dad.

We would have to treasure them in our mind; three brothers would have to hold on to the photographs no matter what was to befall us; they were all we had of a mother, and brothers so missed.

Michael was now reunited with his brothers and father, but soon things would change for him his nice life with Auntie was over, he was now in a different environment where the simple things were scarce.

Michael told us dad was broke. When picking him up from Birmingham, he didn't have enough money for the train fare back to Liverpool.

Michael said they boarded the train at New Street station without any ticket then on arriving at Lime Street station in Liverpool father was faced with the ticket collector, as he approached the collector my father soaked the ticket he'd used to get himself to Birmingham in spit and held it between his teeth, he then picked Michael up with one arm, and held his suitcase with the other, he then offered the ticket to the collector direct from his mouth, the startled ticket collector not daring to touch the spit-soaked ticket waved him on.

Once out of the train station dad told Michael there was a woman who was going to look after him, her name was May, and that he should be nice to her, in the next breath he asked Michael if he could have some money from his piggy bank to buy her some chocolates.

Michael agreed, and chocolates were bought.

With cooking facilities being shared in the dump of a house in Queens Road mealtimes were far from regular.

This gave May an excuse not to cook, instead, she would give us money saying "There's money chips don't come back till nine o'clock give me and your father a break."

We accepted this and could only hope that things would improve as it wasn't what we'd expected. This was the start of not seeing much of dad.

Being young kids, we did not mind being outside living off chips, but on really cold wet days when we had to come home early, we wouldn't have been in for five minutes before May would say, "Come on, get to bed give your dad some peace.

Sometimes we'd be in bed as early as six-thirty listening to the sounds of films on TV coming from their room, films like the forerunner to the jungle book, the 1937 film elephant boy which starred Sabo, family films we would have loved to watch together as a family unit, but May did not seem to want to allow us that simple pleasure.

May was becoming more and more controlling, always wanting us out of the house, or in bed never in the living room. The strange thing was our father never intervened. To our horror, he was leaving May in complete control.

May fully understood Danny as the oldest brother was sussing her tactics, and complaining to my father of her always wanting us out.

She talked herself out of that situation by telling dad, kids are better off outside in the fresh air, she also knew she would have to sort my brother out because he wasn't going to let it rest.

The opportunity arrived one day for her to start her weird evil ways when taking Danny shopping for clothes, she chose the worst of everything whether too big or old-fashioned you name it she picked it.

Danny objected strongly to what she was trying to make him wear. He was now a thirteen-year-old teenager, and like most teenagers were starting to feel self-conscious.

The clothes in question were second-hand clothes sold in a market called Great Homer Street. We had become accustomed to wearing second-hand clothes during our time in Liverpool, it was not the clothes, but her choices which upset him. Everything he picked she'd reject; she didn't show the slightest care for his feelings. Danny had never had nice clothes since the death of our mother and was not spoiled in any way, she was deliberately provoking him, in the end, he could not take any more and left.

May's attitude towards Danny was beyond belief, and I can only think she must have hated children, perhaps even her own.

Returning home May ranted and raved to my father about how Danny had made a mockery of her.

Later when Danny returned home, she got straight on to him about his attitude to the clothes.

Danny returned insults not knowing dad who had been primed and wound up all day and was listening to their argument

He instantly took May's side, without a word Danny was marched by my father into our bedroom, and beaten with a belt across his back. It had been so severe my father returned later to put iodine on the wounds.

The horror of that beating frightened the life out of Michael, and me, we made ourselves scarce for as long as we could that day, and many days after.

As a father what he did to his son, and how he felt about it I do not know. I can only say that I hoped my mother would haunt him for his actions by waking him from his sleep leaving him in a cold, cold sweat for many nights.

I hoped he would receive at least this punishment for his cruel actions; there was nothing else I could do.

Danny was in bed for days after his beating, when he recovered, he told me and Michael he was going back to Eaton Place to live with Auntie Mary "I'm not fucking staying here with that Bitch".

I observed although dad had beaten him his anger was towards May who had instigated his punishment.

My brother Michael, and I tried to make him stay, but we couldn't stop him. Of all the people in the world it had to be her my father had met if ever we boys would need our mother's spiritual guidance it would be now.

Danny had tried to break May's grip on us, but my father had sided with her and had not listened to what Danny had told him.

Life in 1960s Liverpool was tough even for a child with loving parents, ours was about to become like something from a Charles Dickens novel, the only difference it wouldn't be fiction.

My young brother and I were now filled with fear of our own Father, and May used this fear to her advantage, we were not part of her plans, no amount of chocolate such as my brother had brought on first meeting her was going to melt her heart.

Throughout our entire trauma in Canada, and being split up Michael, nor I had ever wet the bed, now suddenly after many weeks living on Queen's road May started checking our bed in the mornings.

"Danny, they've pissed the bed!" she would shout to my father.

Morning after morning this same accusation would occur, during her screams of disgust we would be confronted by our father and would tremble as we tried to explain. Michael would say "It's not me!" and I would say "It's not me!" he would give us a stern look not knowing which of us to blame, but losing patience with us, leaving us petrified.

Nasty, Nasty Tactics.

One morning I was woken by something cold. I looked up as May was standing over our bed, she immediately shouted out to my father "Danny they have pissed the bed again!" It did not take me long to realise to my horror that she was pouring urine over us to deliberately get us into trouble

I knew from the time with my cousin that if someone wets the bed it is warm, this urine is cold as it enters our bed, what had been happening was pure evil by May.

She had produced the urine herself; May had been wetting our bed then screaming at the top of her voice on how she would have to sort the bed, which she deliberately prolonged.

As dad approached us in a foul temper before I could tell him what she had done, she intervened standing in-between my father, my brother, and I, making out she was protecting us she said "No Danny, leave" – "I will sort this out".

As he turned and left, she whispered in an urgent, scary voice, "You better get dressed and get out of here he's going to kill you"! "Stay out till I come and get you"; ``I will leave your tea in here after you eat it and get straight to sleep", we both nodded, still trembling at what we feared our father's actions may have been.

She now knew she had us where she wanted – petrified of Dad, and doing whatever she said.

Now every night when we came home, we would find some food she left on the floor of the foul room we slept in.

There never was any light to switch on as no bulb was ever fitted, we never knew what we were about to eat until we tasted it.

Left for us would be cold toast, or a bowl of jelly sometimes, a bowl of soggy cereal or carrot, and turnip, which was always cold, and made us gag.

We would eat whatever she left if it was too disgusting, we would throw it out of the window, we had realised through experience any food uneaten would be there the next night.

While all this was happening, there were never any questions asked by our father. We were left to our own devices out of the house, and ruled by May inside.

The neglect we suffered under May's rule showed itself further one day when we noticed something white on our yellow unwashed under vests, investigating we were both shocked to find white lice crawling all over the seams of our undergarments, too frightened to say anything we took them off and threw them.

It was disgusting, and now we knew we were truly being neglected, and yet powerless no match for May, we would just have to carry on in this sorry state becoming less, and less able within ourselves as to how to break this chain of despair, oh how we missed our mother.

We lived for six months in Queen's Road, then due I can only assume to its disgusting state, or perhaps the non-payment of rent we moved in temporarily with Aunt Liz's married daughter Jean, and her husband Albert.

As I've already mentioned Jean was a lovely person, and whilst we were under her roof, we tried to explain to her in secret how May was treating us, although she couldn't put her finger on all of May's sly tactics, she spoke to my father, in doing so easing the mistreatment we'd been receiving from May.

Life with Jean within a very short time was to go very wrong which would lead to us leaving the safety of her house.

Jean had a baby boy of about two or three months old named George, one evening she had to go out, and asked May to look after the baby, as the baby had a slight temperature, she warned May not to bathe her son.

May did not heed Jean's words and took it on herself to bathe the child.

The next day Jean woke to find her baby son George dead. "I only gave him quick wash" "May kept screeching" Jean was too distressed to Care, and would only say "I want you out" I don't know how much May contributed to baby George's death, but all her life Jean who has now passed away God rest her soul swore it was because of May that she lost her son.

Thankfully Jean went on to have three beautiful Brownrigg; daughters. Jeanette, Michelle, and Jacqueline.

Very soon after this tragic event Michael and I traumatised once again left the shelter, and protection of Jean's house, and moved to a Tenement estate in an area called Garston.

Near the Tenements were the Bryant and May match work factory, and John Lennon Airport.

OH, SO COLD TIMES

The area we were about to live in was fifteen or so miles away from dad's family, very remote especially for us as young kids, it felt like we had moved to another planet, and any contact with brother Danny was lost.

The flat given to us by the council was number 27D Speke Road Gardens. Each block in the estate had four landings, ours was at the very top, each tenement had different names, ours was known as "the swing park" due to it having swings adjacent to our block.

From the first day, we moved in before getting to sit and enjoy our new home all we would hear from May's mouth was, "Get out", "go out", "go and play".

My father found a job in the area working for Garston Gasworks; he would leave home at seven in the morning, and return after five.

May kept the flat in tip-top condition, and on his return from work she would have a bath run with his dinner waiting the TV switched on in their bedroom, and my brother and I ordered out.

There was no TV in the living room to enjoy, even if there had been May would not have let us have that small pleasure.

We were never allowed in the living room after she had mopped newspapers on the floor. No one was allowed to enter or disturb her pristine housework. Without a doubt it became obvious to us that May's tactics were designed to keep us apart from our father, it was clear she would see to it that for my brothers, and I there would be no home comforts, and certainly no fond memories in this home.

As time passed May's brainwashing intensified, always she battered our heads with threats of what dad was going to do to us.

The words kill us were one of her favourites, she made up stories such as money was missing, a cup was broken or we had been seen throwing stones, and that our punishment was going to be harsh when our father caught up with us.

The list of reasons she gave to keep us scared and away from dad was endless, but looking back expertly, so much so that if we saw our father walking down the road, we would run and hide.

She even had close neighbours believing we were nothing but trouble, excusing the way she treated us in their eyes.

On top of the torment from her, we also had the added problem of a gang of local lads wanting to beat us up, just because we were new to the area.

We were always on our toes ready to run or hide either from dad or the gangs. It was like we were living in the Wild West and we were the only ones without guns. Everything seemed so dangerous at that time.

The only person who in our naivety we would turn to for help was May, we would hope she would have some small amount of compassion, but there was none, not one ounce of that compassion, the compassion we so needed, all she did was add more fear into our heads and make out she was being kind by giving us a small amount of money to keep us barely fed.

People have asked me "how could you let this happen? you should have gone to your dad", we were children tormented by a mad evil woman with no humane feelings you only have to look back in history at a man named Hitler to understand the power of brainwashing, constantly ear bashed we were like putty in her hands.

As days and weeks went by, she would tell us, for example, to turn up near our tenement block at four-thirty if we wanted to eat, as we approached our tenement, she would be standing on the top landing watching for us.

"Wait there!" she would shout she would then throw sandwiches four stories down wrapped in a carrier bag, no matter what she would never forget to shout, "You have your food now disappear before your father sees you" "he's going to kill you" "come back at ten o'clock", wait on the stairs and when he's asleep I'll let you in."

The food was never exciting, jam sandwiches or just plain bread and margarine, sometimes cold toast; many times, we picked the mould from the bread or threw it to the birds.

If late we received nothing dad was home, meaning we kept well away.

Her brainwashing made us believe she was our only hope, that she was protecting us, so evil was she.

She was unrelenting. I am sure looking back if we had stood up to her, she would have killed us by slowly by poisoning, or pushing us from a window of the fourth-floor flat, we could sense this from the mad look in her eyes which seemed to turn white whenever we expressed any desire to tell dad of her sick actions, we so needed help, but all we had was hope.

One day my brother and I found a quiet piece of grass to kick a ball on to each other May had provided the ball certainly not out of any kindness, it was just another reason to get rid of us, concentrating on the game we did not see the gang of about seven lads' approach the very boys who were making our lives a double misery.

“Give us a game,” one of them said.

“OK,” I replied, having no choice; it was either let them join in or get beaten up.

The one with the big mouth organised two teams, I was picked to be on his side thankfully all the days at Auntie's staying out playing football paid off – I was far better at football than any of them, although smaller I was faster and stronger, or maybe just more determined, after the game the one with the big mouth seemed to like the fact he was on the winning side, he asked our names and said:

“See you here tomorrow”.

It now seemed our life in Garston would improve at least with the local kids of roundabout our age, among the older kids in Garston was a breed of teenagers who opened the eyes of younger kids to a world of pure violence, as any poor sod from outside Garston could testify to.

Many times, over the years my brother and I would have no choice other than to fight our corner such was life in Garston there were always plenty of bullies looking for easy targets they didn't find one in me while standing back to back with my brother, and we held our own against the odds many times.

For example, the time I was attacked by a kid twice the size of me I somehow ended up on my stomach with my attacker on top of me, he then started to slam his elbow into my back, after the third blow I thought I was going to die every bit of wind was knocked out of me, one more elbow in the back would have done for me, thankfully Mitch had seen the danger and kicked him off.

Mitch was a nickname I had given to my brother from a monkey character in a children's TV program called Supercar; despite our miserable existence we still had humorous moments, we had to have some humour not to would have to lead our downfall any weakness shown would have been pounced on by the local bullies, we had to stay strong we couldn't give up.

One time without explanation May took us to a house away from Garston to an area called Halewood, she then said, "While I go into hospital." "You will be staying here."

She had arranged for us to stay in foster care for three weeks making sure we wouldn't get any contact with dad; her reason for going into hospital was never explained.

At the foster carer's home, we were given pyjamas, shoes and a new school uniform supplied by the council. We spent those three weeks at a different school in a place not far from Garston called Speke; my brother was so upset during this time he admitted to wetting the bed at night.

When it was time for us to leave the shoes, uniform and pyjamas were taken from us, we were then given back our now-washed raggedy clothes and worn-out plimsolls. Back at the tenement our torment became worse and worse, we were now reduced to waiting for hours of each night for May to let us into our home, quietly she would open the door to let us creep to our room, she would make continuous disgusting Sniffing noises so our father would not hear us enter.

These loud sniffing noises were used by May countless times as we were ushered into our miserable dark room.

God knows I hated her sniffing nose.

How we slept in that room so many times without our father knowing we were there is a mystery, how he never heard us cough snore toss turn, or creak the bed, and not decide to investigate is unbelievable, it was as if in this small flat the door to our bedroom did not exist, not once did he realise, we were there.

From time to time we would hear him through the wall asking May where are boys "they're staying at your sister's," she would reply "they don't want to be here." he seemed to just take her word, he never checked with his sisters, and his sisters never visited him due to their dislike of May.

With no one visiting it meant May was in full control. With no mother, a broken seemingly uncaring Father, distant Aunties, and Uncles, and no involvement from Priests, Nuns, or Welfare officers to tell of our plight we were left under her total insane cruel control.

As time went by my brother, and I became real street urchins.

For years I can't remember having a bath brushing my teeth, or underwear. I do not remember having any underwear apart from the lice-ridden ones my brother and I had discarded when living in Queen's road.

Unless desperate we kept well away from what was supposed to be our home. We both realised to survive we would have to split up as night approached.

We were like dogs hanging around with different mates hoping to get invited into their homes for dinner, and begging them to ask their parents if we could sleep the night.

The state we were in thin, and weedy unwashed hair longer than the Beatles dressed in filthy clothes plimsolls falling off our feet – meant usually being refused entry at any time day or night, but in desperation we never stopped trying, sometimes hearing the sharp "NO!", telling us to go to our own home, this hurt for two reasons 1 we knew we would have to rely on May which would mean a long night freezing on the stairs, and 2 for us there was no home.

Aged nine and eleven what we had not realised until we were older was under May's influence, we were without fully realising it homeless.

Consequently, we were always thinking of how we could get through the night, it was an utter torment in our heads, we would always be encouraging our friends to camp for the night in summer or winter.

Not far from the tenements at a place known locally as the cast-iron shore, this is where we'd always camp; it was a barren area running alongside the River Mersey. The shore leading to the water was a thick black mixture of sand, mud, and oil. If you put your foot in this foul mixture you would sink quite quickly something like being in quicksand added to by all the chemical factories nearby.

The area stank of all sorts washed up on its shore from dead cows, and any other animal you could think of.

Just up from the shore were some small cliffs, it was on this firm ground where we would camp on many a summer, and odd winter night it was a remote dark scary dangerous area never checked on by the police making it a place kids, and adults could take their catapults air rifles, and in some cases twelve-bore shotguns.

One time when we were below the cliffs with two or three mates, we heard something whistle past our ears, we realised some idiot up on the cliffs was shooting an air rifle towards us.

On realising this we ran as fast as we could to get away only stopping about half a mile down the shoreline when we thought it was safe.

However, whoever it was must have followed from up above under the cover of the bushes, as we stopped running ping! we heard a pellet fly past us again, this time we ran for our lives far from the area.

Even with all the negatives of this barren area, my brother and I always kept on at our friends' camp out, making them think it was a wonderful idea, also encouraging them to bring food ensuring we would be fed.

My brother and I became experts at encouraging camping, and as a result, we camped many times, and ate fairly well, beans on toast our favourite meal.

Typical of the English weather most nights we would get soaked to the skin, the poor-quality tent only holding off the rain for a short period, always it seemed to be at the unearthly two or three o'clock in the morning that it would rain bringing camping to an end.

Our friends would return home to their warm beds leaving my brother and I deflated and freezing on the stairs of the tenement, all we would be left with was the hope our mates would not forget about us, and that we would be sneaked into their home when their parents were asleep.

Sometimes if lucky we would be granted entrance by our friends, to avoid their parents we would sleep under their beds, many times I slept in an airing cupboard of a friend John Putterill, it was a terrible experience, but better than being caught by their parents, and turned out into the wet freezing night.

A lot of times we turned out cold and wet. At these times I felt soulless, empty, lonely and lost, and yet I had to stay strong for myself, and Mitch.

Many times, we would be caught by their parents and told to go home, little did these parents know a home was a place we did not have, the shell they thought we lived in was where no help was to be found, May would have locked up the flat for the night without a second thought leaving us to our own devices no matter what the weather conditions.

May knew she had put enough fear into us of our father that we dare not turn up and knock at her door, she could sleep soundly while my brother and I exhaustedly huddled together and froze on one of the many cold staircases within the Tenements.

Always hungry, always in survival mode one time my brother Mitch recalls being in a mate's house as it came around to teatime, there were six kids in this family plus the father and Mitch all sitting down watching TV when the mother of the family came home with a large bag of fish, and chips.

Mitch was sitting in the middle of the kids, his mouth watering at the thought of the meal he was about to receive.

The mother started to pass the wrapped portions down the line until one of the portions reached my brother, he started to unwrap the sweet-smelling fish, and chips and about to tuck in when he was stopped in his tracks, "Hey, what are you doing"? "they're not for you pass them on"! Such was his embarrassment Mitch wanted the floor to open up and swallow him.

To top it off he had to sit there watching as they polished off their meals.

He was then shown the door being told it was time for bed, as the door closed on him he said he felt so hungry, and at the same time pathetic, however, what hurt him was how cruelly he felt he had been treated, he felt he had been set up and behind the now-closed door of his mate's house they were all having a laugh at his expense, needless to say, my brother searched out a new mate.

During one of the worst winters in England in 1963 the snow and slush lay on the ground from November of that year until April of the next, always feeling so cold we wore wellingtons all through that winter, and such was our predicament we were still wearing the same wellingtons in the warm August weather.

The wellingtons left us sore with red rings around the calves of our legs from the constant rubbing, how we survived those winters at the age of (by then) eleven, and thirteen years old is a miracle, we constantly had to find new ways to keep warm, sleep, and eat.

Many times, we both took shelter in public toilets. Stooping so low it was a small wonder we never encountered any paedophiles although I can assure you, we had many close shaves with some strange people.

I wonder had we gone permanently missing if anyone would have asked about our whereabouts. That's how low, and uncared for we felt, and had become.

It was during that harsh winter that May had promised my brother, and I a bicycle for Christmas, needless to say, it was a cruel lie there was no bicycle, and our only memory of Christmas during our life under May's wicked control.

As time passed not the best situation to be in, but far better than the street Michael found a friend whose mother was an alcoholic, he was hardly ever stopped from staying at this friend's house – perhaps only when she didn't have a drink ejecting him from her house as her nerves took over, then very soon being back on the drink becoming forgiving for her actions, and allowing stay.

For me Michael having somewhere to stay was a blessing in that I did not have to worry over him too much.

I for a good ten months found refuge in a school called Blessed John's in Garston which luckily for me, and unknown to the school there was an unsecured window that led to a cupboard of mops and buckets.

I made little space for myself although uncomfortable on the hard floor. I used to feel so fortunate as I approached my secret place, being warm was all I asked.

Unfortunately, one morning I heard the keys of the school caretaker opening the cupboard door, as he entered, and saw me lying there his eyes almost popped out of his head. Immediately he slammed and locked the door shouting "I am ringing the police!" he must have got a real fright, I don't suppose he realised I was only a kid and he could have dealt with me himself.

I left by the open window I had entered thinking in annoyance to myself "that's the end of a nice sleeping space" knowing now the window would always be locked and wondering where next I would find somewhere to keep warm and Sleep.

I rarely attended school as you may have realised if you are struggling through some of my grammar.

I think during the four years of secondary school my attendance would not have been any more than six months at best, going to school wasn't a priority while in constant survival mode, also my brother, and I being humiliated by teachers in front of classmates for our unkempt appearance contributed to the major part of our secondary education being lost.

Looking back, any attempts made by the school to discover the reasons for our lack of attendance or our neglected state would have been swiftly sorted by May with some excellent excuse she would cook up keeping them from her door and stopping father from finding out we were near the area, such was her cunning and her lies.

When we both did attend Heath Road school it would only be on certain days when we needed to be somewhere out of the cold and rain, or when swimming was on the timetable.

Every time we went swimming before entering like any kids, we'd be made to wash our filthy feet by the attendant.

Our feet were always blacker than those of other neglected kids, and we were always spotted by the attendant, embarrassingly we would be ordered to wash a second time, we'd take the embarrassment in return for a rare chance of some fun.

On one occasion my brother Michael was getting dressed after a swim with a party of kids from the school when he noticed in the cubicle next to him a lovely pair of leather shoes, he looked at his worn-out plimsolls, and decided to make a swap.

He walked out of the swimming baths feeling as proud as punch, he had not had a pair of shoes for years just wearing these other boys' shoes was to him like winning the lottery.

Although young he was old enough to know he had done wrong by taking the shoes, yet couldn't stop himself. Leaving his useless filthy plimsolls in exchange for the shoes would lead to his return to school being called into the headmaster's office. "Where did you get those shoes?" the headmaster asked, my brother straight away realised he had been caught red-handed. "I am sorry Sir"; "I just couldn't help myself" "I took them because I needed them"

Thankfully the headmaster realised this to be true especially as he had seen the worn-out plimsolls left in return.

Sitting in the headmaster's office while my brother was being questioned was the mother of the boy whom the shoes belonged to, She asked my brother to take the shoes off, then out of her bag she produced a pair of brand new plimsolls., "Here, son, you have them", "I can see by just looking at your socks you need of them". "What kind of mother do you have" "to be in this state"? she asked.

"I don't have a Mother" my Brother replied. The lady did not reply to his words, perhaps stunned at his reply, then after a brief pause, she thanked the headmaster, took her son's shoes, and left.

The head told my brother he should never take anything that didn't belong to him, and that he must write a hundred lines repeating over, and over again, I must not steal.

Strangely this was the only time anyone had asked about our mother or showed any sympathy towards us, even more strangely we never mentioned our past life to friends, or schoolteachers, although this might have been to our advantage in gaining the sympathy we so needed, sympathy like my brother received from an unknown mother with a kind heart.

Without a doubt our father's refusal to speak of the past made us stay silent, and in reality, we were too young to realise that if people had known of our plight it would have I hope helped us.

Life was so hard whilst surviving at that time we almost forgot we ever had a mother. At times when I was really low, I would think of happier days in Canada and hoped someone in Canada knew of us, and what we had been through, and what we were now living through, I prayed and hoped they held a candle for us, and one day would come to our rescue, my belief in this was strong, and it helped me think there would be an end to the torment we were enduring.

Throughout our time in Garston apart from the odd bottle of milk from a doorstep in times of real need we never took to any stealing as some kids did, it wasn't in our make-up. Luckily for us, there was a market in Garston on Tuesday, and Fridays selling everything a modern supermarket would sell today.

Staying off school we would help the marketers unload their vans in the mornings then help set up their stalls. In the evening we would pack up their stalls, and load their vans.

The wages we received helped us to feed, and clothe ourselves.

There was always a bargain to be had in the market, chips with a big Dundee biscuit was our main food for years, and always within our reach thanks to the wages we received every Tuesday. And Friday.

Mitch and I were always there eager, and ready to work, as work meant staying healthy for Mitch, and me.

Being reliable helped me build up trust with one marketer apart from having me help him on the market. He asked me to babysit his two young children in the evenings, luckily this happened quite often.

Babysitting improved my living conditions greatly. I was given a room. Their house opened my eyes to a different lifestyle, the house had central heating, wall-to-wall quality carpets, a fully tiled bathroom, and cupboards packed with food.

During my nights of babysitting Mitch would often pop in and sit with me enjoying these luxurious surroundings, surroundings not envisaged by us, or many people during the 1960s.

Aubrey and his wife enjoyed this good lifestyle all due to the large income made from running market stalls, selling mainly kids' anoraks.

The sixties were a very buoyant time to be a marketer. I worked for them for 6s 6d a day and 5s for babysitting.

I abandoned school and took to working full-time on various markets for this couple, and became almost a permanent resident in their home for over a year.

Aubrey and Mitta were Jewish, but not strictly religious he would often send me to get him a bacon sandwich from the market café saying "don't let anybody see you give it to me" as quite a lot of the stallholders were Jewish, and would not have approved as pork is forbidden in the Jewish faith.

I worked on the market for about two years, it built up my confidence in dealing with the public. It also gave me an insight into the care most mothers took in their children as they proudly inspected the way their children looked in the anorak or coat they were about to purchase for their kids.

It was at times like this I would think of my mother, and the many times she would have felt so proud of her five sons seeing how smart they looked in the clothes she had purchased, but alas this wasn't to be.

All through my time working at the market I still had an inbuilt fear of going anyway near what was supposed to be my home, May's evil ways, and my father's inactions influenced mainly by her, stopped me in my tracks

Even though I was getting older, and a little wiser, her evilness made me stay well away from 27D Speke Road Gardens during this period.

By the time I was fifteen years old my days working on the market came to a sudden end. Aubrey had started an affair with a woman from his local Conservative Club his wife found out and tried to make him see sense, he didn't listen to his wife's pleas and continued to put the new woman before her, and his children.

His cheating led to a decline of his business and the loss of his house, and a divorce. His wife's last words to him were, for the rest of your life be happy with your new partner, but when one of you dies, you will feel the pain you have given me.

The last I heard of him he wasn't happy he had ended up working for the Ford Motor Company for far less than in his heady days as a marketer when he'd achieved £200 to £300 a day, now he was on an average car factory wage of £25 a week.

The course he took in his life meant I had lost my job, and the roof over my head; it was back to survival mode for me, for him all that was left was to reminisce.

Now older I decided rather than rough it on the streets again it would be best to return to my father's sister Aunt Liz, it had now been over four years since I'd left the safety of her house.

She lived about fifteen miles from Garston, when younger my brother, and I felt it was much further away.

My aunt welcomed me back into her home and was sympathetic, cursing May as to my reasons for needing somewhere to stay, she said she had wished she had been able to intervene over the years, and we left the conversation at that.

I was soon prompted by my aunt to get a job, and rightly I now had to pay my way if I was to stay and be looked after.

One of my aunt's neighbours told me of a job that was going not far from my aunt's house, a company named Rosenblatt's. I went along, asked for a job, and was started immediately.

The Company made household furniture, and my job was to unload wood daily from the wagons then take the wood up the many flights of stairs to the various craftsmen on the different floor levels.

It was hard work. I was surprisingly fit and eagerly took the hard work in my stride, my first week's wage was £4, about average for unskilled school-leavers in 1965. Returning to Auntie's on a Friday evening I told my aunt of the wage I had earned from work, and asked her how much she wanted for my keep, she said, "Give me £3 10s, and you keep 10s." I thought that was a bit steep, but never having had to pay for my keep before I gave her what she wanted, and took my disappointment on the chin so to speak.

The second week at Rosenblatt's I was asked to work Saturday morning as overtime for this extra work I was paid £4 10s, 10 shillings extra for the overtime, telling my aunt of the extra money was a mistake on my behalf because on hearing the extra money I had received she took £4, and once again left me with 10 shillings by taking more money she also left me feeling hard done by, but I said nothing as a roof over my head was more important than arguing over money.

On the third Monday I turned up for work only to find the factory had been destroyed by fire, and I knew my time working there was truly over.

Returning to my auntie's I told her what had occurred, she seemed agitated, and a little annoyed on hearing this "Get down to the dole", now known as the job centre she ordered. I left her house that Monday morning feeling very upset and never returned.

I did not have any knowledge about the dole or how it worked which she may not have realised, now I was a teenager. Maybe being ordered about was not to my liking, or maybe I just couldn't take the pressure of being scolded and was in no fit state to handle it.

My confidence was very fragile and my aunt did not think of this when dealing with me, without thinking of any consequences I jumped on a bus back to Garston, I was like a dog returning to its owner no matter how it is treated, in my case with the need to be near my Dad, and Mitch.

Once on the bus I didn't have a clue what I would do next to find a roof over my head, in my mind I was wishing the bus journey could go on, and on, but in reality, one, and a half hours later I was back in Garston.

It was pouring with rain when I stepped off the bus outside Garston tenements. Within minutes I was soaked to the skin, my shoes squelched as I walked through the various blocks looking for someone who might invite me in out of the rain, but not a soul was about. In desperation, I headed for my father's, and May's flat, I didn't think of it as my home. As I approached the closed door it felt like I was going to knock on a stranger's door, and would be shouted at for disturbing their peace.

This was one of the few times if any I can recall knocking, normally May would always be there waiting to sniff, and sneak us in, or tell us to come back later.

As I stared at the door which should have been a haven, instead there was only fear and mistrust. It took a lot of courage for me to knock that day.

As the door opened May's eyes nearly popped out of her head, the blood ran from her face making her turn ashy white "What are you doing here?" she said before I could answer my father appeared "Get in here and get dry," May was really surprised by me unexpectedly turning up, she moved from room to room like a cat on a hot tin roof, all the time mumbling something under her breath, there were no harsh words from my father which May had always led us to expect he was overjoyed to see me. When May began mooching around with a duster in her hand my father bellowed to her "Make something to eat, never mind bloody dusting!" then he asked me, "Where have you been all this time?" "Where is Michael, and Danny?" I told him where Michael was staying, and I hadn't seen Danny since he left Queen's Road,

"Why are you never here?" he asked, I started to tell him all about what May had been putting us through, as I spoke, I could see the anger welling up in his face as he glared in May's direction.

Before I could tell all May intervened. "I am sorry, I will be better!" Tears flowed down her face she hugged me and then tried to hug my father he pushed her away "I want my kids here," he told her "or I will kill you"! I want to see them here every day ``"Yes, Danny" she replied. "I am sorry, I am sorry," she said as the tears continued to fall from her eyes. I was starting to feel sorry for her, then like something out of a horror film when my father was not looking, she looked at me her face changed it screwed up her eyes became white and wide open, she then mouthed silently "I don't mean a fucking,' word." I was shocked, and could not believe what I'd just seen. I didn't know if I could or should tell my father what had just happened fearing he would have perhaps killed her.

Inside my head, I screamed in frustration at not being able to handle the situation, I felt crushed as to why May was so evil after seeming so remorseful.

Over the next few weeks, the tension in the flat was terrible every time my father was out of earshot May would whisper "I want you fucking out." Sometimes she would change her tone and beg me to leave offering me money to help me on my way. Also, Michael would turn up now and again which drove May even more insane making the atmosphere unbearable.

One evening I was with some friends in a local cafe when an older friend appeared, he said he had just got a job driving a coach, and would I and a few others in the cafe like to go for a little ride around the block.

We all climbed on board, and off he went, the average age of everybody who boarded apart from the driver was fifteen.

A couple of miles down the road the coach was stopped by the police, we then discovered the driver didn't work for the company, he had stolen the coach.

All on the coach were arrested, taken to the police station, and after being ticked off by the police one by one the various parents turned up to collect their kids and allowed to go, all except me, I was told: "Your mother wants you locked up – she's fed up with your behaviour."

May had lied to the police saying she was my mother and refused to collect me, as a consequence of the report she gave to the police saying I needed punishment, and that she didn't want me home, until I was punished, as a result, I was given two weeks in Risley Remand Centre Warrington.

It was terrible you were locked up for twenty-three hours a day.

To show their power as a prison they ordered me to get my hair cut, this was done by an untrained inmate, uneven chunks of hair were taken, and left on my head making me feel ashamed of my appearance.

Once while I was walking down the stairs in the prison one of the prison guards playfully made a boxing spar move towards me, as I responded jokingly, he gave me a hard belt across the head and told me to never put my hands up to him again.

I was not through choice or any real wrongdoing I was amongst some of the weirdest prison officers, and kids you could ever wish to meet.

My time in remand taught me to never get in trouble. It was so bad there, I preferred it on the street.

My father once again was ignorant of what May had put me through, my being missing for two weeks to him just seemed normal.

During our long intervals away, father suffered a minor heart attack, when 44. He seemed to have recovered ok, but true to form May piled guilt on to us for his condition, saying we would make his condition worsen if we stayed at home.

She indicated we would bring about his death. Once again with her mind games, she had the upper hand Dad had left the gasworks and was now working for Ford Motors in Halewood.

In all the time he had been back from Canada he had never missed a day's work, it must have been something in his childhood upbringing that made him this way, and as tough as Eaton Place was, he must have been afforded some guidance in life by his mother, in contrast to the little guidance he was giving his sons.

During the short time staying with my father, I was sent by the dole to two of the worst jobs ever, one. was for a small firm who made wooden garden fences, my job was to dip the wooden slates in coal tar creosote, and throw them three at a time into a stack all treated, and ready to be made into fence panels, no hand or face protection was provided just a pair of overalls, consequently my hands and face were burnt by the creosote, and this was made worse during summertime with the sun beating down agitating the chemicals more than normal on my skin.

Dad advised me to leave this job, and look for a better job.

My next job was in a Company called Evans Medical they produced aspirins, and all sorts of other tablets, my job for them was to mix two powders in a machine which then hammered the powder into tablets, unfortunately, I was not on the aspirins long before I was moved to a part of the factory called Mothaks where mothballs were made.

The smell of mothballs got into your skin, and no matter how many times you washed whenever you were outside of work people could smell the mothballs on you. The only good thing to come from that job was that your clothes were safe from being attacked by moths.

After work on returning home, I had to put up with a constant stream of abuse from May.

One weekend after such a long time I met up with my eldest brother Danny, and told him of the miserable life persisting with May. He told me there was no way I should live like that, and it would be best if I left, and joined him in London.

Danny was now living in London with a woman he'd met whilst revisiting the people who had put us up when we had first arrived in London.

After his short visit, he gave Michael, and myself his address which was West Green Road in Tottenham, and said: "think about it and come down, there's no life here for you." At that time, I didn't know my way around Liverpool, never mind London, but Danny had given me an idea of a way out, which eventually I would take up.

There never was any improvement living with May. She was up to all sorts to make life a misery, once when I was going out for the evening my father lent me one of his shirt ties. It was during the time grandad shirts were all the fashion for men, a fashion that was no more than a collarless shirt accompanied by a cardboard collar.

The struggle I had getting the tie, and the cardboard collar to sit right was extremely difficult, after sweating for ages I finally managed it only to find I had the fat end of the tie the wrong way round "Sod it," I thought there was no way I was going to go, through it all again so decided to tuck the fat end into my shirt, and leave the thin end on show, then off I went on my night out.

The next morning May stood in the hallway screaming "Look what he's done to your tie!" as I came from my room she threw the tie at me. I couldn't believe my eyes the fat end of the tie had a huge cigarette burn right in the middle of it. This couldn't have happened to the tie, as it had been on the inside of my shirt.

I was speechless, my father just looked at me shaking his head, and saying nothing which left me with the feeling that he was disgusted with me, without any proof, and an atmosphere you could cut with a knife it didn't seem like it would go down to well for me to say May had done the damage, I just had to suffer the blame, and let her win again.

She was relentless one evening when my father was working nights. I remember it was a cold night as I entered the flat after visiting a friend. It was in total darkness as I went into the kitchen. There was May with her head in the gas oven "What the hell are you doing?" I said. "I'll kill myself if you don't go!" I left her there, my head buzzing not worried for her as there was no smell of gas, it was just a pathetic hoax on her part but left me feeling petrified at what she might do next.

And as sure as eggs are eggs a few weeks later when I had returned from a night out with friends on entering the house I met May, she was shouting at me at the top of her voice using the most disgusting foul language imaginable saying "We want you out, don't we Danny?" referring to my father who I knew was in his bedroom, her mad rant went on non-stop for a good three minutes, all the time referring to my father, making out he was part of her foul abuse.

All through her ranting never once did I hear my father's voice, upset at what was happening I closed the door to my room drowning out her voice, and couldn't wait to fall asleep, and dream "reality was a nightmare".

The next morning, I met my father. "Hi son, are you OK?" "Yes, Dad" I replied not one word did he mention of the previous night's screaming from May.

I soon realised she must have drugged him with medication, perhaps sleeping tablets he had been prescribed, to think how close to death he might have been that night showed May's evilness was never to end, and a tactic perhaps she had used before. These two episodes would finally force me to leave,

I could not cope anymore with May's sickening ways, she must have hated the thought of doing the slightest thing for us children, maybe the abandonment of her children as part of the reason for her cruel treatment, or she was just purely insane? Throughout our time under her influence she only used threats towards us, never once raising her hand, I can't for the life of me understand what pleasure she got from the way she treated us.

Throughout her time with dad, she was like a cat on a hot tin roof, never relaxed, forever planning ways to keep us away from our father.

I sometimes wonder if she knew my father before he had met my mother and was jealous of the life, they were embarking on in returning to Canada, and her revenge was now being taken out on my brothers, and myself, but these few words are just my thoughts in not understanding why people like May walk this earth unscathed.

I was now seventeen, and all my thoughts were of my father's lack of concern for me, and my brothers which now I realise were the result of May 'influence, he was like a light bulb long blown still hanging there, but shedding no light, he was switched off from the reality of life, and the needs of his surviving children, he had bottled-up events, and demons he needed to deal with.

Due to my father's heart condition he and May were offered a small two bedroomed flat in Halewood – 47 Blake acre Road.
It was designed for pensioners, and certainly not suitable for families, they took it without hesitation, this at least meant my father would no longer have to climb the four stories of stairs to their tenement flat, which the doctor at the time thought was putting a strain on his heart.
The small house was in an area with gangs of threatening teenagers on every corner, which made the likes of me a newcomer to the area feel very insecure, along with May's disturbing ways, which I knew would never end, made up my mind to search out my brother in London and try to make some sense of my life.
My first duty was to visit my brother Michael who was still staying with his friend in Garston, at that moment in time he was working in a large factory called the Tan Yards; it was a stinking place to work with the smell of rotten cowhides filling the air for up to a quarter of a mile away.
His job entailed cleaning the flesh off the hides of slaughtered cows which is the first stage in the process of making leather. "I'm going to London, Mitch," I announced. I told him I had had enough and was going to take a lift to London to be with Danny. Mitch needed no more explanation he was, and still is the only person in the world who had lived, and suffered the horrendous six years of being controlled by May, worrying day after day how to survive never shown one bit of love, crawling with lice not a picture together or a birthday remembered, or a Christmas to recall,6 years largely spent freezing on cold concrete stairs huddled together to keep warm, chilled to the bone with teeth chattering in clothes that wouldn't keep you warm on a summer's night, let alone in the depths of winter,6 years of our life from the ages of 8 and 11 onwards to, fourteen, and seventeen left homeless because of this evil woman's endless brainwashing, living in filth feeling so pathetic at having to wait until way after midnight to then have to sneak through the door like thieves while listening to her unearthly Sniffs
Entering a cold undecorated room containing a solitary bed without sheets just old blankets rough to the touch, and itchy on your skin, sleeping in filth always, hungry begging like dogs feeling ashamed, petrified, and unable to comprehend, defend, or understand why.

Of the time spent existing under May's influence, we had found our way of surviving. It's impossible for Michael, and I do remember how many times for 2,190 days we sneaked into our room, camped, took refuge in a cupboard, froze on a staircase, or how many miles we clocked up wandering the streets of England's cold wet unforgiving climate.

How we never succumbed to severe illness is a blessing, we had now passed this hurdle and were now on our way to becoming men.

MOVING TO LONDON

While waiting for a car to stop. We both mulled over more unanswered questions "Why," Mitch asked, "why are we not sure if dad cares about us?" "I think he loves us," I replied" "Do you think he knows we love him

His questions kept coming "Do you think we are too much of a reminder of that night in Canada? And why do we allow May to control us? and why he said "Why, Rob, "has this extra stressful life been put onto us after all we've already suffered?" adding being separated almost nine years from Danny, ending with why had our father come back after abandoning us in Canada only to abandon us again.

I tried as best I could to answer his questions "I think he loves us," we love him, and wanted to tell him to snap out of May's spell, but You know we just can't overcome her cunning". In my heart, I knew Mitch would join up. I felt It was meant to be. I had no real answers for Mitch. He was my younger brother, and I wanted to give him answers, but I was as lost as him as to why all this had happened.

His last question chilled me to the bone, why when I was living with Aunt Violet and had a chance at a decent life had dad taken me from that life if he knew he could not match it. I told him he thought he was doing the right thing in bringing us together and without May's interference, it would have been so different.

I continued telling him we were now becoming men and what we had been through must be for a reason, I told him that in many times of deep distress I had prayed to God, and cried out to something within me for help, and we must have a guardian angel or else we couldn't have reached to where we were now.

I firmly believed there had to be an angel –there was nothing else, no other answers. I have tried my best to describe a chapter of the life my brothers and I endured.

The emotions and inner experiences dealt with as young children are almost impossible to fully describe.

We never asked for much, just to be children, loved, and cared for, but simply without our mother's protection, we were denied that simple pleasure.

As I thumbed to the passing traffic eventually a car stopped.

My life's journey was to continue, and I was now on my way out of Liverpool. "You have Danny's address," I said to Mitch. "When I get sorted, I will be in touch." We hugged each other, and as I left, we both had tears in our eyes. I was on my way, and there was no turning back, with nothing to turn back to.

I knew Mitch would join up. I felt It was meant to be.

After getting several lifts, I was finally dropped off at London's Euston railway station, my lift told me I was not far from Tottenham, shattered after a seven-hour journey it was around two in the morning, I now had some time to kill as London transport was not fully under-way until 6 am, and holding me up from making my way to my brother.

It felt strange being in the huge train station, it was quite warm with now and then a draught of stale air rising from the tube station below. I thought to myself "This must be the smell of the big city", and I quite liked it. I was seventeen, and as green as grass, in other words very naïve, I didn't fear what lay ahead. It couldn't be any worse than what I had left behind.

Being accustomed to roughing it, I figured out the best way I could get through the night was in one of the many telephone boxes inside the train station, I entered one of the phone boxes then pretended I was making a phone call so I would not be disturbed, gradually I fell into a dose while standing up, my legs annoyingly buckling quite often disturbing what little sleep I managed to get, but I was so tired I persisted until eventually opening my eyes fully in the early morning at just about the right time to continue my journey.

That first day in London was an eye-opener I had never seen so many people rushing around in my life, I was directed to the part of the Tube station which would take me to Tottenham by a kind woman who was the first of about twenty people who had at my request bothered to stop, and help, as she left I was still confused about the underground system being my first time of using it.

Travelling the tube was a daunting experience for a first-time traveller like me. I was travelling for hours up, and down and every other wrong way until finally, I arrived at my destination Seven Sisters Tube station as instructed by Danny.

When I turned up at Danny's address, we were both overjoyed to be with each other. Danny who was now twenty years old was living with a thirty-four-year-old woman named Ann who was an unmarried mother of two girls.

He had been in London for just over a year and had been living with Ann for about six months.

During the first week of my stay, Danny familiarised me with the area of Tottenham which was so different from what I had known in Liverpool. In the evenings we would go to the local pubs which were always rocking with different bands blasting out their brand of music.

I was not accustomed to drinking, and after having two or three pints on returning to Ann's house the beer would always leave me with the sensation of the ceiling spinning, a feeling I hated.

Not long into my stay, Ann started to complain stating Danny, and I were not behaving very responsibly, and she had enough to deal with her two daughters, and me being there was not acceptable.

She was not nasty in any way and we understood her point of view, she told Danny "Your brother will have to leave," and said she would allow a week for me to find somewhere.

It was at this time in my life I realised the true meaning of brotherly love. Danny told Ann he felt she was being too harsh, and that he was sorry but there was no way he could turn his back on me, he would be leaving with me.

We left Ann's before her weeks' notice was up without anywhere to stay, but Danny assured me we would have no trouble renting a room as various shop windows displayed rooms to let in the area

The adverts went something along the lines of "room to let an address" with the price per week given, "apply by phone" we phoned room after room only to be told "Sorry it's taken" or "References required".

As the day rolled on, we became more and more concerned as to where we were going to find somewhere to stay.

During our window shopping for a room, we struck up a conversation with two lads from Wales who were in the same predicament.

They told us they had been trying to get a room all day without any success, as we were all in the same boat, we struck up an immediate friendship and put our heads together to try to work out a solution.

One of the Welsh lads had heard of a hostel in Peckham called the "Spike" which had over 1000 beds at its disposal for homeless men, and if you turned up without anywhere to stay, you would be given a bed for the night.

This seemed to be the short-term solution, so all four of us all decided to head for Peckham lads being lads. We didn't rush stopping at a few pubs and leaving it late before jumping on the Tube train to Peckham.

The Tube journey was long, none of us had realised Peckham was on the south side of London miles away from Tottenham in the north.

When we arrived at Peckham station it was close to midnight, we asked for directions and were pointed towards the hostel, and told it was one hell of a walk from where we were, with no buses running this late at night all four set off.

After walking for over an hour we were stopped by the police. "Where are you boys off at this time of the morning?" one of the officers asked.

"To Peckham Hostel – we've nowhere to stay and have been told we can get a bed there for the night." The response from the police officer was in these exact words – he said, "words of advice when you arrive there tie your shoelaces to the bed, and stick a cork up your arse" as they left, we were all stunned at what he had said, but fully understood the meaning.

Tired with no choice we carried on and finally arrived at the hostel with the words of the policeman still ringing in our ears.

We weighed up the surroundings at the hostel but didn't like what we saw there were all sorts of sad people in the queue for a bed, winos tramps down and outs you name it, all looking desperately in need of a wash, and a good night's sleep we lined up waiting to fill in forms asking your name last address place of employment if employed, and so on.

Once through the form-filling, you would be given a towel, and soap then made to shower before being shown to a bed. After a couple of hours without even getting to the form-filling we decided this place was not for us and left thinking it best to restart our room search.

Seeing those poor men in the state they were in, was a wake-up call for me. I had been like them in Liverpool for years, please god not again no way did I want to be like them now.

I worried without any education, and no home, this life could be a continuation of my past life and my future fate.

We returned to Peckham Tube station feeling shattered and made our way to the Circle line then boarded a train happy in the knowledge it was a tube train which went around, and around all day without a break.

Once onboard, we were all fast asleep within minutes, we slept soundly right through the morning rush and must have looked at a strange sight all four lined up like we didn't have a care in the world, although in reality, we had more worries than most traveling the tube that day.

After sleeping for a few hours on waking we changed trains and headed towards North London to an area called Tufnell Park.

Danny knew this area was good for flat hunting, as soon as we left the Tube station, we came across a shop which had a large number of postcard advertisements in its window telling of single or double rooms, and flats to let.

Any flats advertised however were well out of our price range, and were maybe more for families.

Our search was for a double room. Danny picked one out at an address just off Holloway Road. The advert read, "Double room to let, shared bathroom, no cooking facilities, apply in person to landlady 50 Anson Road London N7."

The two Welsh lads took the option of a different address.

On the way to check the rooms we agreed on, if we did, or, didn't get settled we would meet up in a pub we passed called the Hercules.

We then split from the Welsh guys wishing one another luck.

Danny and I arrived at the advertised address and were greeted by a friendly Irish woman who showed us to the room. “It is £8 a week plus a week in advance. Do you want to take it? Without hesitation, we agreed Danny paid her the full amount.
She then showed us the bathroom, gave us the keys and said if we needed her, she lived at the side of the house.
After she left, we were ecstatic, it was quite a big room on the 1st floor of a large house, the room we rented had a door which led to a walled garden, it was pretty basic, and yet after some of the places, I had laid my head made me at least feel secure and being with Danny safe.
There was no home comfort all it consisted of was two single beds, which you had to supply your sheets for. There was a metre which you had to feed with coins for your electric light and heat, a small sink in one corner of the room for face and hand washing, there was no TV or radio, making the room just a place sleep which was all we needed during a time of beggar can’t be chooser, we just felt blessed to have a bed, and a roof over our heads.
The next day we were given a rent book; this was a passport to getting some money from social security. In 1967 you could walk into any social security office with a rent book and tell them you had just arrived in the city were looking for work and needed money to tide you over for rent, and food.
You would have a long wait, but in the end, they would pay you in cash. Once established every week you hadn’t found work you would get a cash hand-out: just enough to pay the rent, buy your food, and maybe enough over for a few pints of beer.
With no cooking facilities in the house meant always eating in cafes dotted all around the Holloway area.
After eating to escape the boredom of our room I didn’t hesitate to follow Danny to the pub
It certainly wasn’t boring in the Hercules; people were from all over the British Isles, I had read comics like The Hotspur Lion, and Eagle in the stories I had read about these nationalities fighting wars together and how well they got on.
I soon learned it wasn’t really like that, the dislike some narrow-minded people had of each other just because of a different accent, or skin tone was baffling to me.

Largely due to the Beatles' popularity in the sixties Danny and I being from their home town Liverpool made us quite popular, due mainly to our accents being similar to the famous four of John, Paul, George, and Ringo, one of their big hits forever on the jukebox at the time we frequented the pub, was, "Hey Jude".

At the back of the pub, there was a large stage where a talented Irish band performed every weekend, they insisted on playing nothing but Beatles songs.

The lead singer Mick was mad about Paul McCartney and always tried to emulate him, and such was the power of the Beatles in the 60,s when he and the group heard my brother and I was from Liverpool they would always want us to sit close to the stage so as they could listen to our accents.

Then during intervals without success try, and copy our unique accents.

Danny and I did not have strong Liverpool accents due to our time growing up in Canada, but our Canadian twang was fading fast.

Sitting in the front with the band had its advantages as most weekends towards the end of the night all hell would break loose behind us, with chairs and tables flying. I was no stranger to violence after living in Garston, but what I was discovering in the Hercules was in a different league.

One example of this was a fellow Danny and I had got to know quite well, a thin six-foot guy about thirty years old from Liverpool, named Tommy.

I liked him because he was softly spoken, but what I will always remember of him was his eyes. They always looked so sad but considering what he told us had happened to him in the Hercules I was amazed he wasn't sad and crying every day.

He told us one evening outside the pub he had a bit of an argument with a drinking partner over a girl which neither of them had any success with.

Tommy said the argument developed into a fight that wasn't serious due to them both being drunk and hardly able to stand up, during the fight he had got the better of the other guy with no real hurt caused to either of them.

After the scuffle they went home, the next day Tommy told us he was sitting in the pub when approached by the guy he argued with who said "no hard feelings over last night Tommy." Tommy replied "Fair enough no hard feelings from me either" and offered him his hand, they both shook hands then the Irish fellow asked him what would you like to drink "A pint of bitter," Tommy replied the chap went to the bar returned with the pint and said "Here you go, Tommy." then smashed the glass into Tommy's face.

Tommy then turned his top lip over showing us a large scar left by the attack I had always thought up until then he naturally had a thick top lip.

As the guy attacked Tommy pulled his head back in doing so the glass went through his top lip. His story made me think I should always be aware as I was growing up fast to a different abuse that could befall me.

I knew almost straight away I would have to move from this kind of life, but for the moment I would have to put up with it, there was nowhere else to go.

I was now seventeen and Danny twenty, ten years had passed since our time in Canada, we had not lived with each other apart from those few weeks at Queen's Road, and yet in most respects, it was as if we had never been apart, such was our brotherly bond.

During my time with Danny away from the pub our discussions turned to our prospects and how we could improve them, the obvious answer was to get jobs we even talked about joining the French Foreign Legion if life didn't improve.

Many nights I would say to Danny "Tomorrow we get up early and look for work" that night Dan would be full of enthusiasm and raring to go, In the morning when I approached to wake him his attitude would have changed from the night before, he'd be in a mood, and the more I tried to encourage him to get out of bed the worse that mood became, In the end, I gave up trying to persuade him.

Danny would sleep until four or five in the afternoon, as I got older I was never very good in the mornings, and nor was my other brother Mitch, although sleeping late may be normal in most teenagers, I sometimes wonder if after the traumatic events in our lives sleep was a way of blocking out the reality, especially at times when there seemed no way out of the structureless unguided existence we lived in, it seemed better to sleep, and dream.

I now know for some time my brothers and I were all in a deep depression, without realising it.
Depression to us was something older people got, therefore not taken as seriously by either of us.
The more I got to know my brother the more I understood he was a deeply hurt soul, all the tenderness that was shown to him during his first ten years as the first-born, then the loss of his mum and then his grandmother soon after, added to the lost affection and harsh treatment from our father would have affected him mentally much more than Mitch and I.
When I looked at him deep in my thoughts, I would find myself feeling so sorry for him. I sort of dismissed myself from any consciousness of being in the same situation and looked at his life from the outside and it wasn't a nice picture.
I should have hugged him, but a hug was something we had both at that time in our lives forgotten the feeling of, also forgotten was the meaning of such actions, I suppose life being tough we felt we had to be tough, but deep down we longed for simple affection. Danny was 5' 1" in height. I sometimes wonder if the shock of life had stunted all our height, He had dark brown hair with a small bald patch near the crown of his head about the size of a sixpence; this was due to an accident that occurred when he was a toddler.
I was told when he was a baby in Eaton Place hot fat had been dropped on his head burning his scalp and that his hair would never recover its growth.
People compared his looks to Robert Mitcham the Hollywood actor.
Danny was a straight-talking person who expressed himself with plenty of swearing, anyone who knew him took this with a pinch of salt, one minute he would be cursing at you because he didn't agree with you, and then once you explained your point, he would be full of apologies.
He was a person who read a lot and enjoyed gangster films. He loved being a Liverpool 'Scouser', and he was proud of his Irish roots from way back in time.
Due to the cruel events that blighted his life, Danny had a bit of a chip on his shoulder, which would show itself from time to time, he would get very annoyed if anybody commented on his size.

Many times, I intervened to prevent the situation from turning violent and to perhaps save my brother from trouble when odds were stacked against him.

As for me, I carried on looking for work and as time went by found myself a job bagging carpets in a warehouse.

The job entailed putting a carpet in a plastic bag to which an address was attached, the carpets were then sent off to various customers.

The pay wasn't good, but much better than trying to live off social security payments.

Danny had trouble getting out of bed, limiting his chances of finding work, therefore he was always short of money.

With the money I was earning I supported him on nights out. One night we met with our Welsh friends in a pub near by.

Over some time, we went on to have some good nights together having a drink and listening to music.

As Danny and I had quite an easy-going landlady some weekend evenings after the pub closed, they, and maybe a few other friends we knew, would come around to our room for a late drink.

On one of those weekends I returned to our room early feeling a little ill and fell asleep, later that evening Danny and the Welsh lads entered our room from the garden door well and truly drunk, each carrying a box "Look what we've got here!" Danny said, in the boxes were bottles of the Greek alcohol called ouzo, they laid them on the floor and then said "Let's go back and get some more" "Where are you getting them from?" I asked "there's a van outside with loads in" one of them replied.

Returning with the second lot of boxes unknown to them they were seen and followed into the room by several policemen "Right you lot are nicked and you in the bed" meaning me "get dressed."

As they took my brother and the lads out, I protest my innocence telling them, "you can see I was in bed and had nothing to do with the theft." After a short discussion, they told me I was lucky this time and left.

Danny and Welsh lads were kept in custody over the weekend all appeared in court on a Monday morning and received prison sentences.

Danny, having some previous minor charges from his time in Liverpool was sent to Pentonville prison for three months, the Welsh lads were sentenced to two weeks.

I told Danny I would stay in the area, but due to the police incident the landlady had given me notice to leave, and on his release, he could find me in the Hercules, there were no mobile phones in the 1960s; this was our only way of meeting up.

I was given a week's notice by the landlady to leave.

I was quite upset at leaving as I had grown familiar with my surroundings, but the landlady was adamant she wanted me out in her mind we had all crossed the line.

Now on my own, yet more familiar with how to go about finding a place to live, I soon found a room in Mercers Road still in the Holloway area.

My new landlady was Irish but far stricter than the previous one.

She had rules, such as no noise, no drunken behaviour, and strictly no girls. The room I rented was at the very top of the house furnished with a bed, and a wardrobe. It was a tiny attic room clean and tidy with one window looking out to the road below. There was a large shared kitchen where from using it I got to know some of the other men who rented rooms in the house.

Most were Irish and worked for a large building firm called Murphy's.

They were nice men which made the house quite pleasant to live in.

None in the house could cook apart from at best tea and toast.

They kindly showed me the best cafes in the area which were far better than the cafes Danny, and I had discovered.

I continued to frequent the Hercules pub of a weekend, making a few friendships as I went along.

MEETING LINDA.

On one of the weekends, I sat with a guy I had got to know over a few weeks when two girls sat down near us and said hello.

One of them we knew from the pub was nicknamed Fanta, a nickname cruelly given to her for being a little overweight.

As we chatted, she introduced us to her friend Linda.

Linda was a pretty blonde girl whom my friend immediately seemed keen on, he chatted to her all night buying drinks for her and Fanta, and I at the drop of a hat, so keen was he to impress Linda.

Only on the odd occasion when he went to the toilet did he and Linda break from talking to each other.

On one of his trips to the toilet, I did manage to speak a few words to her not saying too much as I was quite shy, my experience around girls was limited to a brief episode with a girl called Audrey and Lynda when I was about fourteen and living in Garston which consisted of a little kiss and cuddle.

At the end of the night, the guy I was with offered to take the two girls home by taxi and he asked me to come along, I agreed.

On arriving where they lived in Hornsey, I was astonished when on leaving the taxi Linda leaned over giving me a long lingering kiss. It happened so quickly I was shocked, and at the same time overjoyed.

Both girls were then in a flash saying goodbye and at the same time saying they would see us next Friday in the Hercules.

On the journey back to Holloway I was gobsmacked, the guy who was with me even more so as he had made all the running to impress the attractive Linda.

Back to Holloway he hardly spoke a word and after that night I never saw him again.

As the week went by I more or less forgot about the incident, I had thought what had happened in the taxi was her way of letting the guy know she wasn't interested in him.

On that next Friday I didn't go to the Hercules for what reason I can't remember that following Saturday morning I was in my room when I heard voices coming from outside, as I looked out of my window I spotted Linda walking away from the house, as I stared down she turned looked up saw her face lit up, I gave her the thumbs up and went to meet her.

I was truly amazed at her appearance on my doorstep; fate had dealt its hand once again.

She had got my address from someone in the Hercules, she said she had knocked and been told by the landlady no one named Robert lives here.

With what she'd been told by the landlady she was about to give up on me, that one glance out of the window, and chance to see her was about to begin the next chapter of my life.

It was wonderful having a girlfriend; she was great looking, and right from our first meeting I was walking on cloud 9. I knew I had found someone to love, and hoped she would feel the same about me.

From time to time we sneaked into my room avoiding the landlady and talked till late at night. On one of those nights, she declared she was going to stay the night.

The next day she thanked me for being a perfect gentleman and not trying to make any moves on her. The next time she stayed she made the first moves.

It was at this time I first found out about the birds and bees.

She kept a diary with a code word for every time we made love. The word was coffee. Both young people were not very good at making it but always enjoyed it.

One time she took me to her auntie's, while there I went to use the toilet and overheard her say to her aunt "He's gorgeous, isn't he?" It didn't feel big-headed. I honestly just thought to myself "God, she likes me! I felt confidence surge through me, a feeling I am sure everybody needs, for the first time in years her comment made me feel good about myself.

At times I would jump on the bus to where she lived, as I would get off the bus, she would be waiting for me running towards me arms outstretched so glad to see me. On seeing this I was smitten and I went head over heels in love.

During my courtship, Danny was released.

I introduced him to Linda. He got on well with her, and as he could see we were both mad about each other he suggested we leave the area of Holloway and look for a room somewhere near to Hornsey where she lived.

I took Danny's advice and found a nice room in Hornsey run by a Greek gentleman. The house overlooked a really beautiful park, called Priory Park, the area much nicer than Holloway, greener and less built up.

Linda lived on the other side of the park at 134 Middle Lane with her parent's brother Clifford and Sister Brenda, as time went by, she introduced me to her mother and father, her father was a small stocky man five feet tall who loved opera and was himself an excellent opera singer.

He quizzed me on my job prospects which at that time I did not have.

Linda and her father both worked for social security in the very office I had received social security payments for when I had first arrived in London.

Subsequently, Linda informed me she, and her father had looked up my file and the comments about me were not good, I had been described as a hopeless case that would most likely never hold down a job, needless to say, Linda's father advised her not to get involved with me, believing what he had read to be true, also he thought because of my lack of education her future would be better served elsewhere.

I had only been in London for six months, and yet someone in the social security department had passed such a harsh judgement on me, I could understand their reasons as I didn't have one shred of evidence of my school day achievements, no proof of past jobs nothing, therefore I could understand her father's concerns for his daughter.

As for Linda's mother, I think she may have liked me a little, but deep down hoped her daughter's relationship with me might quickly fizzle out.

Linda was too keen on me to take notice of her father's advice, or the report by the social security department. She believed in me when I told her I would prove whoever wrote those degrading comments about me was wrong.

I quickly found a job with Islington council unfortunately for me it was a fair way from Hornsey. I would have to take a twenty-minute bus ride to Finsbury Park then jump a Tube to Old Street station, from where I had a ten-minute walk to the baths located in Ironmonger Row, a pretty rundown part of Islington.

The building I worked in had a public swimming bath, also a Turkish bath, plus public laundry facilities; I was employed in the laundry Department.

It was a nice old building built in 1931. My job in the laundry was to make sure everything ran on time. It was an extremely busy part of the baths with a constant stream of women booked in to do their weekly wash.

Most women did not have the strength to drag their washing from the large washing machines and to then pack the large industrial spinners, to keep things going smoothly I would do it for them, it was extremely hard work, but for helping them I was rewarded with tips which boosted my wages nicely.

I worked a week of early days from 8 am till 5 pm, and a week of late evenings from 2 pm till 10.

My problem was I always had trouble waking for the morning shift and would always be trying to get to work on time.

As I was so hopeless at getting up in the mornings in the summer of our first year together Linda used to walk across the park on her way to work to give me an early morning shout, but soon got fed up when the winter set in.

I managed on my own in the end.

Although it was always a struggle.

On Saturdays Linda would meet me after work, all the staff at the baths were quite impressed at how good she looked.

One fellow from my home city a guy of about forty years gave me his advice, “She is really lovely”, “but I warn you”,-you” will have trouble holding on to her” I took his advice with a pinch of salt thinking to myself “She thinks the world of me what does he know?”

One Saturday after work about 5.30 pm Linda and I set off for Old Street station, as the train to our destination pulled up the carriage, we boarded was jam-packed with lots of people sitting, and standing, as we looked up and down the train there were only two places to stand at the end of the carriage either side of the doors.

Linda stood on one side, and I on the other, as I had been on my feet all day, I pulled down the guard seat and sat down.

Then as I looked about the train I noticed seven, or eight West Ham football supporters all standing further up the carriage, all of a sudden two of them made their way down the train and stood next to me and Linda, one of them stood in front of her the other stood in the middle of the two of us, as Linda looked at me I could see the fear in her eyes, with my finger I beckoned her to move towards me, as she moved the guy in the middle thrust his lower body towards her making a sexual “ooh” noise.

I left my seat feeling disgusted at what he had done to my girlfriend whom I dearly loved and doled out my punishment.

Without thinking I punched him square in the mouth, he yelped and ran with his accomplice back up the train.

I knew now for sure there was going to be some serious trouble and I needed to think quickly because within seconds in a single file the seven of them started to move towards me shouting how they were going to tear me apart.

The biggest of them right at the front, I felt sure someone on the train who had seen what had happened would come to my assistance, how wrong I was, not wanting to get involved people on the train aware of what was going on were scurrying like mice through the door at the other end of the carriage.

I knew as long as I kept my back to the wall, they could only get at me one at a time, as the big guy got near to me, I struck up a boxing pose."

To my relief seeing my stance he stopped in his tracks slowing the others down, to get anywhere near me they now had to scramble over the seats. In my mind, I was praying for the train to hurry to its next stop.

I kept them at bay as best I could, and then, at last, the train pulled up at a station, I grasped Linda by the hand and we both jumped off the train, luckily, they did not follow they just shouted abuse until the doors to the train closed.

As the train pulled away, I looked inside, other than the rabble I had fought off there was not one passenger left in what had been two full carriages.

I learned a valuable lesson: London was a mind your business kind of place.

Linda was so proud of me for defending her, as I went to sleep that night, I felt my guardian angel had looked after us both that evening, not for one moment thinking as some people suggested it was due to luck that I didn't receive a scratch.

As time went by to save me the gruelling tube ride to Islington, I bought a scooter from a shop in Edmonton north London.

On the day I purchased the scooter I handed over the money and was given the keys to my chosen scooter. I was then left with the problem of how to ride it, I could ride a bicycle so balancing the scooter was no problem, my main concern was I didn't have a clue how to change gears.

I didn't know what first, second, third, and fourth gears were meant for, with no regulations to abide by apart from learner plates I was off.

How I got from Edmonton to Hornsey that day without crashing I will never know, I must have had some strange looks each time I changed gear and wobbled along the busy roads from Edmonton Tottenham Wood Green, and finally Hornsey.

With plenty of practice I worked out the gear changes which made me confident enough to use the scooter for getting to work. I was over the moon having no need to Tube, or bus to work anymore.

After about six months I woke up one morning, got ready for work, stepped outside and was shocked to find the scooter was not there, it took me a minute or so to realise it had been stolen. I was gutted I couldn't understand how it had been taken as I used to wrap a large chain around the wheel and padlock it. I immediately went to the police to report the scooter stolen.

The officer behind the counter took the details of the scooter and told me more than likely bolt cutters had been used to remove the chain.

He then said he knew of a thief who previously had stolen a scooter, and might be responsible for the theft of mine. He gave me the address of a house in Priory Road to check out and possibly retrieve my scooter, adding "Keep it to yourself I told you this" I took his advice and went to have a look.

On arriving at the address there was no sign of the scooter I was just about to leave when I decided to pop my head over the garden wall and there was my scooter being stripped of all its chrome parts by a young lad, I shouted at him "Hey you, you thieving swine".

On seeing me he went white and ran into the house, I asked a woman standing on her doorstep nearby to ring the police.

I then banged on the thief's door and he wouldn't answer so I shouted through the letterbox "That scooter better be around my house tonight", or ``you're in real trouble." Just then the police arrived.

The police knew of him and called his name, caught red-handed and opened the door. They forced him to push the scooter the short distance to where I lived.

As it was now in bits and unusable before they took him away, I told him he had better put it back as it was, or I would come looking for him. His name was Malcolm Brown, surprisingly about two days later he turned up at my house with a mate. "I've come to put your scooter back together." "OK," I said, and true to his word for two or three days he turned up putting back everything he'd taken off the scooter.

He was a person who didn't say a lot, although I did find out from him his court date for the theft. I watched over the days as he put things right on my scooter and wondered if perhaps, he had had a poor start in life, maybe similar to mine, and my brothers, so feeling sorry for him I decided to give him a letter for court explaining what he had done to make amends.

I left it at that and hoped my letter would make whatever sentence he received more lenient. It must have been around two months later that I went to my scooter and was shocked to find all of the chrome parts missing once again. Straight-away I thought, "Bloody Malcolm Brown!" Also thinking "Surely not after what I've done for him!".

He no longer lived at his previous address, but I knew where his mate lived taking a chance I went to his mate's house and banged on the door, as the door opened he was standing there with his mother, I shouted at him "If Malcolm Brown doesn't have what he's stolen from my scooter back to me soon I'm coming after you" I then turned and left. I was not sure if Brown was the culprit, or not, but two days later my suspicions were proved right, there was a bang on the door and as I looked out of the window, I saw Brown running away from the house, as I opened the door there on the step lay all the parts belonging to my scooter.

It must have been eighteen months later that I walked into one of my local pubs, I hoped to bump into my brother Danny, as I looked around, I couldn't believe my eyes there serving behind the bar was none other than the thieving swine Malcolm Brown. Now Brown was to pay to some degree for what he had done, I just stood in the middle of the pub where about thirty men were having a drink and at the top of my voice shouted "Listen to me – see him behind the bar, a warning you all to watch your change, and you" meaning the manager – watch your till because him" – pointing, at Brown – "he's one thieving bastard."

The pub went deadly silent as I turned and left; just the sight of Brown had made me feel sick.

The next day I returned to the pub if need be to expose him again, thankfully Brown had scarpered mercifully that was my last sighting of Brown.

Without a doubt, he was a person who had the devil on his shoulder and is to this day I would think still making hard-working people's lives a misery.

During my time in London, I had made friends with a chap from Liverpool who was about to visit his family for a weekend and offered to take me. This was a great opportunity for me to visit Mitch.

I took up his offer, Linda decided she would like to come, so on a cold winter's day all three of us set off. It was around about November-time and pretty cold, twenty miles up the road he declared the heater in his old ford popular van wasn't working making the journey horrendously cold, but the anticipation of meeting Mitch outweighed the discomfort

Arriving in Liverpool I met up with Mitch and encouraged him and his friend to get to London where there were plenty of jobs, jobs far better than their present one in the Stinking tan yards.

The Weekend visit was short, before leaving I asked my friend if we could stop off at my father's, to tell him Danny and I were doing ok.

I introduced my dad to Linda and in a private moment asked him what he thought of her "she's all right, but don't marry her," he replied.

His words left me bemused, I just shrugged them off and never went into any detail as to why he felt that way, yet thinking about it to myself, I realised it was not long ago I had heard similar from the guy at work and I wondered what my father and the workmate meant.

Knowing we were not staying more than an hour and would soon be 200 miles away in London. May was civil, although ashy white during our short visit.

Back in London during our courtship Linda and I had often spoken of the future and how we hoped one day to have a baby in our life, both wondering what colour his, or her eyes might be.

It had only been idle talk that became a reality, Linda was pregnant, she was eighteen years old and understandably petrified at what her mother and father would say.

I told her I would stand by her and not worry. yet deep down I was petrified of what her parent's reaction might be.

Very soon I was to become a dad, and not sure of how I would handle this huge responsibility, being so young. Neither of us had summoned up the courage to tell her parents, and as the months passed worried that soon her shape would show she was pregnant which they would surely guess, but not what we wanted, we wanted to tell them face to face.

Unbelievably the problem of telling them was to become even harder as Linda's sister Brenda revealed, she was also pregnant.

The dilemma intensified as every day went by, I would say "I'll tell them tonight," "No, no not tonight Linda would say," and secretly relieved I would put it off till another day.

The crunch came one evening when all four of us were saying goodnight outside Linda's parents' house; Len, Brenda's boyfriend was saying goodnight to her and I could not help overhearing him saying "lam telling them tonight." I thought to myself "Just like me he won't do it He'll chicken out." Just at that moment, the girl's parent's car pulled up, and then in a crumbling voice, Len said: "Can I have a word with you"? By the look on Linda's mother's face, I think she knew what Len was about to say. As they all went into the house Linda, and I went to listen by the door the shouts and screams coming out of the house sounded terrible. In a panic Linda told me to go home, and that she would see me the next day.

When I got home, I was in a state. I told Danny what had just happened. His advice was for me to get straight back round to Linda's house and confess to her pregnancy, although scared stiff I took his advice and went back.

I knocked on the door and it was quickly answered by Linda "What are you doing here?" she said with a panicky look on her face "I have come to tell them" I replied "No, no, not now!" The door was then slammed in my face.

I went back home cursing to myself, and feeling frustrated not having resolved what had to be said.

The next morning the weight was off my shoulders the pregnancy had been confessed by Linda to her parents, by returning to her house after she had slammed the door in my face her mother had asked what I had wanted saying "I hope you're not pregnant, too" "Yes I am," Linda had replied tearfully.

That night was a long one in Middle Lane for all of Linda's and Brenda's shocked family. As disapproving of me Linda's parents had become, they now had some serious thinking to do, slowly they started to at least acknowledge me although it was painful for them

They became even more upset when we announced we were going to marry, they tried to dissuade their daughter, try is all they could do she was six months pregnant and wanted to marry, plus a new law had just been approved allowing under-twenty-one-year-olds to marry without parental consent and would take effect from 1st January 1970.

We booked the ceremony and were married on 3rd January 1970 in the Haringey registry office. I was now nineteen married, and yet I had never even been to a wedding before.

Our marriage was a short half-hour ceremony witnessed by my two brothers, Linda's Sister Brenda, her boyfriend Len, plus two of Linda's friends and their partners, all of whom tried to make the occasion a happy one.

Sadly, for Linda no part was played by her parents, reluctantly her father did at least drive her to the registry office, and then as if in some kind of protest remained in his car, closed his eyes, and slept throughout the service.

As for my father, I received no words of good luck at all and wondered if he even knew or cared I was marrying.

After the wedding service one of the guests asked if anyone needed a lift to the Hornsey Tavern pub where we had arranged a few sandwiches, Linda, and her girlfriends declined as they were being taken by her dad, as no one else had a car my brothers and I all gratefully accepted his offer of a lift not knowing he would be pulling up in a builder's open-backed wagon, all suited up we were driven to the pub for a celebration drink.

Our marriage was not by any stretch of the imagination lavish with neither of us having any financial back-up.

We married with all the right intentions, in love, and importantly our child would be born to married parents.

Linda's parents had gracelessly provided Linda and me with accommodation at the top of their three-storied house in Middle Lane. We had a small kitchen, living room and bedroom.

The large house was in a state of refurbishment on every level due to the fact my now-father-in-law was a do-it-yourself fanatic who seemed to start but never finish a job the house was too big for him and his limited skills.

I would have loved to have assisted him and shown my thankfulness for the accommodation but due to my inexperience, I was not much help to him in sorting out the many jobs that needed finishing.

The three months leading up to the birth of my child were quite eventful. Mitch had moved to London with his friend who was nicknamed "Foggo" both were put up by Danny in the room I had vacated, I carried on working at the baths in Islington. Informing the manager Mr. Booth that soon my wife would be giving birth and I may have to rush off at any time.

He was a nice man who over the years of my working in the baths had been lenient with my sometimes-poor timekeeping, he was very understanding of my request and told me not to worry when the time came, I could go.

That time soon came around on 3rd April 1970 I was at work when I was called to the manager's office "You had better get off" Mr. Booth said, "We have had a phone call to inform you your wife is in labour".

I rushed out of work and jumped on the first of three buses that would take me to Alexander Park Hospital in Muswell.

Sitting on the bus all I could do was wonder whether when I got there, I would be the dad to a boy or a girl.

I arrived at the hospital at around ten o'clock and to my surprise I was greeted at the entrance by my brother-in-law Len "What are you doing here?" I asked "Brenda has given birth to a baby girl" he replied smiling.

Amazingly both sisters had gone into labour together, and I have since learned there was only a 125,000 to 1 chance of two sisters giving birth on the same day, year, and month.

I congratulated him and naively asked what sex my child was "Linda hasn't yet given birth," he replied.

Once in the hospital I was taken to Linda and told by the midwife to when required to give her gas and air, the screams from Linda during that day were unbelievable, so much gas was used to help her cope I felt so sorry for her, and at the same time terrified, but didn't want to let her know how I felt.

I was powerless to do anything other than what I was told by the midwife.

After many hours the midwife took one look at me and said "You look like you're going to faint go to the waiting room. I will take over now. "As I left, I was totally worn out I blamed myself for her pain, in a daze I did as the midwife had ordered, yet my ordeal was not over while in the waiting room I could still hear screams from Linda, I prayed it would end, then at around 7.30 pm the midwife entered the waiting room "young man your now the father of a baby boy", "you can see him now". "

That first moment I saw my son I just wanted to hold him it was then and always will be the highlight of my life, as good as it gets, there is no other way I could describe my feelings at that precious moment in time, what Linda had gone through during the birth only cemented my feelings of love for her, it was an amazing way to feel.

After about twenty minutes with my new born son I was told by the midwife it was time to leave, she pointed out that Linda and the baby needed to rest which I certainly knew to be true.

Once out of the hospital I flagged down a taxi for the short journey from the hospital to Hornsey, having just become a dad I was elated I gave the taxi driver a huge tip. I then searched for my brothers to give them fantastic news.

I was a dad, and they were uncles, but of all nights I couldn't find them.

I had to tell someone the fantastic news so I called on one of Linda's friends a girl from Manchester called Cathy, as I told her I was a dad it hit home to me what had just happened, it was the best feeling ever a feeling of responsibility mixed with joy, that night I sobbed, and cried my heart out, Cathy put her arm around me in a comforting way and I think she got my personality that night, I felt she knew I was an ok person, and her friend Linda was in safe hands.

We named our son Justin; he was a happy beautiful baby, everything you could wish for.

When he was about two months old, Linda with Justin by her side had fallen asleep, during the night he slipped out of the bed. Linda immediately searched in the darkness feeling where he'd fallen, then panicked, and screamed to me "I can't find him!" I rushed to the light switch and turned the light on and there he was, he'd rolled under his crib and was fine lying there with a big smile on his face, a smile which has always stayed with him and is now part of his lovely character.

His uncles, my brothers Danny and Mitch loved being with him and he loved being with us, he was soon kicking a ball and making us laugh with his funny little antics He'd brought much-needed joy into mine, and my brothers' lives, we even enjoyed our first Christmas meal all together.

Unfortunately, Linda did not like the idea of my brothers being around our flat as often as they were; she felt at the start of our marriage it was giving little time for just me, and her to be alone.

I fully understood her concerns, but could not find it in my heart to tell them to ease off coming around. I tried to explain to her they had no one else in London apart from me, I also knew just like me it was their first insight into home life since Canada which they loved being part of.

I ended up torn as to what to do. I just tried to let things ride and took the constant verbal telling-off from Linda, all I could do was try to prove to her the person I was by being a good father and expressing my love, which she constantly needed.

She would always sit on my lap wherever we were seemingly so vulnerable, always she would say "Am I fat?" "No, you are not fat, you are perfect" I would reply.

She was never satisfied; I tried to help her by always telling her how beautiful she was. Not once since our early meetings did I receive the merest compliment from her, it didn't bother me but sometimes I was left feeling unsure of how she felt about me.

Over and over throughout our marriage the question of "Am I fat? "Am I pretty?" would arise, I felt sorry for her thinking she had such a low opinion of herself and all due to being a little overweight when she was younger.

I boosted her confidence by encouraging her to take up jogging with me which helped her figure and her confidence.

I never let her down, always building her confidence at the time, not realising while all my attention was focused on her, not enough of my time was spent with my son.

SAD NEWS.

Two years into my marriage, on 13th March 1972, I was called to the phone "there's someone called May who wants to speak to you", I felt sick as I heard "that" name I knew not hearing from her during my time in London it would be impossible for any good news to come out of her mouth.

As soon as I answered with no sympathy in her voice May blurted, "Your dad's dead, he's had a heart attack." Stunned I didn't reply I just hung up the phone tears welled up in my eyes and my head spun.

He hadn't been much of a father, but I still loved him and had hoped to have some kind of relationship along with my son, his grandson who he had never got to know. I had tried to generate some spark in him when Justin was just a few months old on a visit to Liverpool. On that one occasion Justin spent the night with him, and as I left, he said he would visit in the future, he never made that visit or a phone call.

To my sad regret he had been back in England for ten years and I doubt in all that time I had spent 10 hours in his company, perhaps a sad reflection on him as a father, but who knows the stress, he felt from his great loss in Canada it may have left him in a deep depression.

This is a question my brothers and I have searched for all our lives, but we are nowhere near to the answer, yet without doubt one thing we know for sure the reason for three Sons and a Father being apart was an inhumane woman, named May.

Although he had suffered a heart attack four years earlier, I never dreamt he'd die so young, just forty-seven. I was twenty-three years old with no fond memories of my father and brothers together, the last picture we had taken together was saying goodbye in Canada fifteen years past.

Now fond memories would never arise, and any information from him regarding my mother's life was lost

I was left to break the sad news to my brothers. They were shocked, stunned, and as upset as me.

My brothers and I immediately left for Liverpool, Linda was to follow and arrive a day before the funeral.

As soon as we arrived, we visited Dad in the chapel of rest, as we looked at him lying there, we realised our loss and felt so sad, also we were aware apart from our young lives in Canada we were never going to fully know him, If I said I had spent a full hour in his company at any one time I would be exaggerating.

Maybe he had died as a person fifteen years earlier on that dreadful night in Montreal. Before the funeral, my brothers and I stayed with a cousin, one of my father's family.

They were a large family of seven kids; in their small house, they somehow made room for us. They knew we could not stay at my father's whilst May was there.

The house we stayed at belonged to Evelyn, my cousin. She had a heart of gold. They were a rough and ready family, something that I had to explain to Linda before her arrival, also telling her the bed we had been given had no sheets and could she bring some from London.

That night we put the sheets on the bed and went off to sleep. The next morning we were woken by four of my cousin's small kids all shouting in unison "Mum, mum, mum – they've got sheets!" I think they thought we were posh. It was quite amusing and I leave it at that.

A few days later dad was cremated in Anfield cemetery, the cemetery was where I had my last ever sighting of May who had stood at the service with no tears in her eyes just a bowed head, none of my father's family comforted her, neither I nor my brothers felt any sympathy for her, and I told her so in the foulest way possible

People were shocked at my words, but knew they were justified.

She had scarred and took away our basic human rights to live anything like a normal life. What she had done would be for all our lives so hard mentally to repair.

I was relieved she would never be part of my life, but sadly never out of my mind. She is best summed up in an incident that happened some months later.

Mitch returned to my father's home in the hope of retrieving some mementos to remember dad by. Also, there was the question of his ashes.

When he arrived, he found the house boarded up, enquiring of a neighbour as to why, he was told: "It was shocking" "as soon as your father died", "she took to wearing miniskirts and held noisy drunken parties", "and because of this she was evicted by the council".

These neighbours' words were of no shock to us – unlike what the neighbours had just found out about May, we knew only too well the real May and were not shocked by her actions.

She stayed rotten till the end, we later found out she had falsely claimed to be our father's wife and had scampered with his death in a service lump sum.

One thing for sure before May meets her maker, she will have to first pass by my Mother but will have no excuses for what she put us, young boys, though, and is without a doubt going down to the fires of hell.

Before Linda and I left for London we were offered dinner back at my cousin's house, but politely refused.

On my return to London, I noticed a lack of support from Linda and her family. Linda seemed to think it more important to tell everyone the story of the lack of sheets, and some unhygienic meat carving she had witnessed which made life a little embarrassing for Me.

It would leave me trying to explain to people not everybody was like this in Liverpool., I felt these family members had tried their best to help at a time of great sorrow and shouldn't be belittled.

Thinking to myself if only Linda knew as poor as they seemed, they had a lot compared to where in life I had been dragged down too. I kept these thoughts to myself. London life was never going to run smoothly for my brothers and me.

Not long after being back from the funeral. Both Danny and Mitch were doing ok, but not in the best of jobs, Danny was working the night shift on the railway which for him was ideal not being the best in the mornings.

His job involved cleaning the tunnels of the soot that accumulated, all the men on that job looked like coal miners at the end of their shift, black from head to toe.

Mitch was working in a laundry that washed white table cloths used for banquets; by Tottenham Hotspurs football club.

They had eased off coming around, they knew it was putting a strain on my marriage, they spent most of their spare time in the local pubs playing darts and watching football, basically just killing time avoiding the boredom of living in a bedsit. Whenever I could I would pop to the pub to be with them.

On one of these occasions both my brothers were drinking with a thin-faced fellow from Glasgow as I looked at him. I remembered an old saying told to me by my father-in-law, the saying went "beware the men with the thin and hungry look" this fellow was a perfect example of the wise saying.

I took an immediate strong dislike to this guy, a dislike I had never experienced before with anybody else I had met. I pulled Danny and Mitch to one side" and said. "What are you doing with him"? I don't like the look of him keeping well away from him" as I left, I repeated my warnings. It was as if I had a sixth sense concerning this man, but with a few pints downed Danny and Mitch thought I was worrying over nothing.

Later that evening I was woken by banging on the door, I answered to find Danny and Mitch standing there Mitch was holding a handkerchief soaked in blood to his face. "What's happened? The bastard hit me across the nose with a bottle, and he's stabbed Danny in the back. My father-in-law and I wasted no time in rushing them to the hospital, where thankfully after being stitched up they were both ok, the doctor commented had Danny's stab wound had it been a little deeper there could have been a far more serious outcome, other than a few stitches, he could have died.

On the way home, they explained what had happened. The guy they were drinking with invited them for a drink. He lived with his father, after a few drinks he started cursing his father who was quite an old man and was scared of his son, Danny who was still feeling upset at the death of our father remonstrated with him, saying "You shouldn't speak to your father like that.

A few minutes later slyly without warning the son of a bitch because he didn't like Danny's point of view, smashed a bottle into Mitch's face, Danny very drunk by now cursed him and started to get Mitch out of danger, as he was going down the stairs behind Mitch, the animal of a human being, stabbed him in the back.

When they were halfway to where I lived the scum of a man ran up to them "sorry sorry lads" he pleaded, they took no chances with this sly rat-looking person this time.

Mitch took aim and threw the blood-soaked tissue he had held to his nose straight into his attacker's face; they then both gave him as good kicking which he deserved, he then ran off, the sly rotten coward he was.

As for my brothers, they apologised to me for not listening to my warning. Their attacker was never seen again in the area, he had run off in case the police visited him. I must admit we had our odd amusing times together in London.

Like the time I was picking up a friend for football training as I waited for him in my car, there was a tap on my window standing there were two pretty girls about eighteen years old "Excuse me" they said. "Could you tell us how to get to the M1 motorway please"?

They were miles from the M1 but intended to walk there then thumb a lift to their home city of Wolverhampton.

It was around seven-thirty in the evening on a dark October night, not a good time for young women to be in this situation.

I assured them my brothers had a place where they could stay safe for the night, and they could then make their way home in the morning, both girls agreed; abandoning my plans for the evening I took them to where my brothers stayed.

On arriving both my brothers were out, but luckily the door was open. I waited with the girls for ages, but there was no sign of them.

I could see both the girls were shattered. I told them I was leaving and would leave a note for my brothers explaining their situation, and if they wanted to sleep, to use my brother's beds.

I then left wondering what my brothers would make of what I had done.

The poor Scottish teammate I was picking up for football training had been bemused when he eventually came down to find me gone when I later explained he understood, and we both had a giggle.

Well when my brothers came home, they could not believe their eyes there was were two gorgeous girls fast asleep, it was to them, and I would think to any young man like a dream come true, ready-made girlfriends.

Happily, the girls stayed with my brothers for two, or three months until one day near Christmas they decided to return to Wolverhampton.

It was a magical time for all four, and I should never forget the girls or my brothers for the rest of their lives.

Also, never to be forgotten, although two years apart, was the time I obtained tickets through my football connections for the 1984 Milk Cup final, and the 1986 FA Cup final, both games featuring Liverpool versus Everton.

Both times Danny and I had a great day out listening to 100,000 people from one city united, altogether proudly before the game singing "Merseyside, Merseyside, Merseyside" over, and over repeatedly. Liverpool won both games, Danny and I both happy with the results left Wembley on those two occasions very happy.

I would have been just as happy had Everton won, I just loved being there with Danny. Considering we never went to any matches during our time in Liverpool to have the luck to go to Wembley for these games was fantastic.

Mitch was gutted he wasn't in London when I obtained the tickets, mind you he wouldn't have been happy as out of the three of us he was the only Everton supporter, and they lost both games.

When my son was about two years old Linda returned to work and Justin was placed with a babyminder.

She had left social security and now worked for British Telecom.

I carried on working for Islington council and hoped a better job might come my way, that chance came when my brother-in-law Len found employment with British Telecom.

When he told me the wage he was on and that he is taught to drive by the company, I became very interested.

He told me they were taking people on and I should apply. I asked him what chance I would have of getting a start.

He said at his interview he had been asked to wire up a bell, and after doing it successfully was given the job.

I immediately applied, and an interview date was given. Len showed me how to wire a bell and I counted the days to my interview full of confidence, thinking I would have a good chance of getting the job now I could wire a bell, I thought if I could land the job how great it would be for my family in providing a better life and if I learned to drive it would open up all sorts of opportunities.

The day of my interview finally arrived, as I waited for two BT employees to introduce themselves. “I am Mr. Rudd and this is my secretary,” they asked me how long I had been employed by the council, I had been there for over two years which I thought put me in good light with them, after a few more questions they then said, “We are going to leave you for fifteen minutes with this maths paper”. Just my luck! To get the job I would have to get at least 50 percent of the maths correct, there was to be none of the bell wiring I had anticipated, how I wished during those minutes I had some schooling to fall back on, for me these simple maths questions were like trying to read Japanese.

I made an effort but knew out of the twenty sums if I got one right it would be a miracle.

Well, that miracle did not happen a few minutes after I’d finished the secretary took the paper away, then Mr. Rudd re-entered the room saying “I am a sorry son, but I don’t think you will be suitable for this job.”,

I just stared at him not knowing what to say and feeling very embarrassed with my maths effort.

As I stared at him, I thought to myself “I’ve nothing to lose. “and said to him “Please give me a chance”, I won’t let you down”, I think a small miracle did happen that day because after a long pause Mr. Rudd said, “OK I’ll give you a chance”.

When I left Telecom House that day I was overjoyed, it felt, at last, I could hold my head up to people who doubted me. I felt proud that Mr. Rudd had thought of me as a decent person, and based his decision on my word, not the maths paper.

Things moved along quite smoothly for me in Telecom, I picked the job up well and gained my driving license; I represented telecom at football, and was happy in my work, also gaining some good mates. Linda, Justin, and I had moved from her parent’s house to a top-floor flat run by a housing trust in Milton Park Highgate, it was a nice flat, and we furnished it well.

It was here that I had my first ever birthday party at twenty-five yrs.' Linda had organised the party as a surprise, as I came home from work that night, I entered the flat and walked into the room to shouts of, "Surprise! Happy birthday! it" Amazed me. I was a bit lost as to how to handle all the fuss which I had never experienced before, I was shocked most of the night, thinking it was someone else's party as things like this didn't seem to happen for me.

I still loved my football and played most Saturday, and Sunday's always wearing number 11, winning lots of trophies. I represented Middlesex and was once asked to attend a trial with Bolton Wanderers.

Playing locally with successes, and new friendships made I didn't go to the football trial preferring family life.

My brothers would always turn up to watch me play on Saturday afternoons; Afterwards, we would return to the clubhouse for a drink, then as everybody started to drift home I would think "Time for me to go" It was at this moment I felt sorry for my brothers everybody else had a home to go to whilst they didn't just a grubby bedsit.

Just as always, we had to come to terms with the situation.

As time moved on Mitch met his future wife Carol on a visit to Liverpool and decided to stay in the city. He did try settling with her in London briefly, but it never worked.

THE BEGINNING OF THE END OF MARRIAGE.

I was now seven years into my marriage and didn't foresee any problems at all. I loved each day being a husband and a father to Justin.

Until without warning, I encountered what must be every married person's nightmare, and a part of my story I have no choice I have to tell.

Returning home one night from work I spotted my wife at the top of the street getting out of a car, a car I had never seen before as I called to her the car sped off.

I didn't think too much about it until I looked into her face, it was almost like a stranger's face staring back at me, with guilt written all over it.

At that moment I felt as if my stomach had dropped right out of me, I knew straight away she was cheating, it was so unexpected without a second thought I told her to leave, my head was spinning I wanted her to say it was nothing and I shouldn't worry, but there were no words of comfort.

As we entered our flat with an air of inevitability, she rang her father to come and pick her up.

I was crushed and choked. When her father arrived, he waited with her in our bedroom as she packed some of her things, I overheard him say to her "Ask him if he will leave his wife before you ruin your life with Robert and Justin". As they left, I was gutted and deeply hurt. Thankfully my son was at Linda's mother's and hadn't witnessed the sad episode.

My son was now my main priority.

To see him I would have to visit him at Linda's parents' house each time it became more painful when I had to leave.

At that time of my life, I could have done with some guidance in any form, but I was on my own.

During my visits, there still seemed to be some spark between me and Linda she would make a fuss of me, and as I was about to leave would linger with me saying "Maybe we can work it out", I didn't want to think about life without my Son and couldn't just turn off my feelings of love for her as easily as she seemed able to turn off for me, and just the thought of not being around my son full-time, or of him ending up with an outsider influencing him, was unbearable to me.

Her words of maybe we can work it out seemed my only choice, plus the fact I loved her making getting back together easy, but in doing so I felt like I was apologising for something I didn't do and making her feel she was special for something she should have regretted, instead she just lapped up the extra attention.

I put out of my mind what had happened and hoped we would once again become a happy family. I had lost over a stone in weight during this domestic trouble, I was not equipped to deal with what was happening, I was too trusting, and forgiving with no one to turn to for advice, my seven-year-old son Justin the most wonderful thing that had happened to me had been unfairly pushed to one side during this sad episode, it was a relief to me, I had secured his future.

We never returned to the flat in Milton Park as it would now only hold bad memories. On her father's advice we decided to stay in his house, and save towards a mortgage. I worked the daytime with Telecom and in the evenings took a job with a minicab company.

I was determined to make things work and kept faith in the mother of my child, but all the time I felt what little confidence I had was draining away. I knew I would never know the truth, and wondered if Linda had taken her father's advice, if she had waited to find what her man friend intended, and had been let down.

Perhaps I was now the second choice. I put these thoughts to one side and trusted in what had always been for me a good loving relationship.

During all this upheaval I had not seen much of Danny, when I did see him, I didn't tell him what had gone on. He had enough on his plate without worrying about me, anyway in my mind I had sorted my marriage out, and so kept it to myself.

The only time I could meet up with Danny was in the pub. There didn't seem to be anywhere else for him to go. It was a sad situation, but something we would always overcome and not worry about as long as for any length of time we were in each other's company.

All through our lives my brothers and I had never run down or picked on anybody whether better or worse off than us, we would befriend anyone who seemed decent and down to earth, although sometimes people would not give us the same respect. That lack of respect was to test me one evening when I met up with Danny in the Hornsey Tavern and found him in a sad mood. "What's up, Dan?" I asked "I had a bit of trouble with the barman from the Compasses; he told me that the barman deliberately kept overlooking him by deliberately serving everyone else at the bar before him.

Danny explained to me he had told the barman in straight-talking terms what he thought of his ignorant behaviour. He went on to tell me after finishing drinking at the pub later that evening he had stopped off for a meal in a local restaurant and as he was eating the barman came into the restaurant saw him and attacked him, saying, "Don't talk to me like that again or I'll fucking kill you!" and slapped him.

I told Danny I felt it was out of order "No," he replied "I wasn't hurt, and I think I was a bit over the top the way I spoke, so let's just forget about it, "fair enough" I replied.

Later that week I once again checked up on Danny only to find him in a distressed state, I asked him what was wrong; the barman has just been in here and given me a few slaps he replied, now I'm no hero, but what Danny told me made my blood boil this was now a case of bullying

The barman was twice his size as Danny, and now twice had laid his hands on my brother, belittling him once in the restaurant, and now in a pub full of people.

I wanted it to stop before it got further out of hand, also playing on my mind was the fact someone had stabbed him in the back not too long ago.

The barman who assaulted Danny was a young Irishman of about twenty-five years old six-foot-tall, with whom I learned a bad attitude towards a lot of people in the area, and next to Danny who was 5ft 1 he must have felt no fear.

I asked Dan if he knew where the barman might be now, "He will be in the Compasses" Danny replied, with that information, we headed for the Compasses.

As we entered the pub, I asked Danny to point him out.

He was drinking at the bar with a couple of other people as I walked towards him my intentions to defuse the bullying with a bit of bravado, as I got behind him at full stretch, me being only five foot five tapped him on the shoulder, at the same time thinking to myself "God he's a big lad."

As he turned, I immediately asked "Are you picking on my brother? "He looked around, spotted Danny and said "Yeah."

It was not what I had expected to hear. I had hoped he would apologise and put an end to it, but as he looked down at me, he must have felt he had nothing to fear and turned back to his drink.

The next words out of my mouth were "if you don't leave him alone you will have to answer to me", now I thought he might back down but no – "Ok" he replied "Let's sort it outside then" he banged his pint glass onto the bar and loudly said "Right" as he did this I noticed the strong muscles in his arms, as I walked towards the door with him right behind me I was thinking "If I go outside he's likely to kill me"

At that moment words remembered by my Uncle George flashed into my head if ever you're in the right, and trouble, and there's no way out get in first, also flashing through my mind was the violence I'd witnessed many times in Garston tenements.

With that thought I turned took two short steps jumped like a footballer heading a ball and head-butted him as hard as I could full in the face, he went straight down to the floor, but it still wasn't over he was a strong lad and tried to get up so I grabbed him by the hair and gave him two good punches, this time he stayed down.

I did not feel proud of what I'd done although for my brother at the time I felt I'd done the right thing, there had been no choice. It was a dog-eat-dog situation, something I wish to this day had never happened.

The next day I met Danny for a coffee as we sat in the window of the cafe in Crouch End unbelievably crossing the road and looking right at the both of us was the Irishman both his eyes badly swollen, I thought "Oh no, not again!" and felt sure he would seek revenge. He just looked at us and carried on his way.

A few weeks later Danny whilst on his own crossed paths with the Irishman, not a word was said and there were never any repercussions.

I wasn't put on this earth to teach bullies a lesson in how to behave but without a doubt, I taught this fellow one.

What I had revealed to myself during this incident was my father's aggressive genes had certainly passed to me, and when put into motion produced a different person, thankfully through the mild-mannered genes of my mother I have most of my life under great strain been quite mild-mannered, realising the pen is much mightier than the sword.

Not long after the regretful incident with the barman I had a heart-to-heart conversation with Danny, I told him I thought it would be better for him if he returned to Liverpool with Mitch, to give it a try away from London now he was older and wiser.

I admit to selfishness in what I told him due to the pressure within my marriage, but living in London he was befriending people who were just passing through and constantly moving on and most without good character it was no way for him to live, It hurt me to say what I did, but felt I was being cruel to be kind.

Danny knew I was right and after our conversation went back to Liverpool.

Not long afterward Danny met his future wife, Wendy, giving some justification to our joint decision, of him seeking a better life, away from London.

Now I had to concentrate on finding a home for Linda and Justin, helped by my taxi driving, and living with her parents, both our wages left unspent enough was saved in over six months for a deposit on a mortgaged house.

After a long search, we found a small terraced house in Bath Road Edmonton. It had not been our first choice that had been for a house in Tottenham which at the time was 7,500, we had been gazumped on that property, house prices were rising that fast we later paid £14,500 for a house in Edmonton, double our target.

The house we purchased was in really good condition, and the neighbours were very nice.

There was a school close by for Justin who was now 9 years old and all in all we were very happy. I carried on with my football at weekends, Justin tagged along while Linda loved to shop with her mother, buying pretty clothes and shoes.

At different times I attended Mitch's and Danny's weddings in Liverpool. After Danny married, he moved from Liverpool to Bath, and then on to his wife's hometown of Trowbridge in Wiltshire, Mitch settled in Liverpool with his wife Carol.

As time moved on, I became a proud uncle to my brothers' children, Danny had a son and a daughter named Daniel and Eleanor. Brother Mitch also had a son and daughter named Michael and Vicky.

I was happy for my brothers and also proud that they too had started to buy their own homes, it now seemed that at last, we had all found much-needed stability and happiness.

As for my happiness, just being around my son was fantastic any time. When we could we would be off somewhere in my car, unfortunately, we both missed joining up with my brothers for our fun games of football in the park. Justin loved to sit with me and watch TV programs like Star Trek, and Doctor Who.

Any time we could we would be off in my car to somewhere special. I remember one time I told him off for biting the car dashboard, afterward whenever alone as I drove my car I would smile at his tiny teeth marks staring back at me, and think to myself how lucky I was to have him in my life, also thinking the little teeth marks made my car very special.

From time to time I would suggest to Linda it would be nice to have a little brother or sister for him, I was always met with the excuse of "Oh no, I couldn't go through that pain again", "Or I couldn't bear to put on the weight" she was very career-minded having another baby would have been too much of an Inconvenience, instead she chose a small poodle.

Linda named the dog brandy but nicknamed it pooh. With her commitment to her work, she soon rose the ladder to become a supervisor in charge of wages within British Telecom, as time went by, we both decided as Justin was about to start secondary school a new house near to a good school would be in his best interest. We found a semi-detached property in Cowland Avenue, Enfield, a bit upmarket from where we were which meant a larger mortgage, but it was a progressive step to take and therefore worthwhile.

Things went along just fine; we had nice family holidays in Dawlish Devon, back at home we both worked hard and built up a nice living environment.

As time went by constantly with little reason as to why Linda would return from work in an angry mood making life quite uncomfortable.

I tried to make things better by helping with the housework repairing the car you name it I tried it, soon it came to the point where the strain must have been showing in my face because on one visit to Linda's sister she asked what was wrong as I told her of her sister's behaviour she replied "You want to take a ride up to Telephone House one dinnertime and check her out" When I heard those words my heart sank – please not again. It was five years since her first affair, I was gutted, it felt like my heart had been ripped out, and stamped on.

There was no love lost between my wife and her sister, their children being born on the same day didn't cement their respect for one another, Brenda's husband was the total opposite to me, violent towards his wife, moody, and a drinker.

Brenda went on to tell me my wife was spending her dinner time in the company of a male supervisor from another department of British Telecom. She also gave me his name and told me that he was married.

With that information I found this guy's internal number and rang him when he answered my head was spinning I had no plan as to what to say, I just said: "If you don't keep away from my wife she, and her clothes will be in your front garden you then can sort out with your wife" as to why the clothes of another woman have appeared on your doorstep, I then hung up It left me feeling like I should have done and said more.

I felt frightened that I was losing my wife and son once again the fact he was a boss at Telecom made me feel I was inferior to him, and at the same time trying to hold on to some confidence by telling myself that I was more of a man than he would ever be, my confidence was truly battered.

I had been playing catch-up in life and my marriage for years, and now it seemed I was back to square one.

That night Linda didn't return home. She rang my son and told him she was staying with a friend named Patricia.

For over a week I had no contact from her then one night she rang in a flood of tears begging me to please let her come home, once again I gave in as I thought of Justin now twelve years old the high mortgage we had, and what the alternative would be, I was worn out and could not think straight anymore.

There were apologies galore from her as we somehow tried to repair what little trust there was left in our marriage the truth was I was unhappy and unknown to me at the time depressed I just plodded on I was never a jealous man I had never had anything in life so didn't tend to have jealous feelings, but I was now very insecure in my marriage and didn't feel much of a man.

A good 18 months passed when One day I was working near her office and gave her a ring" I was told. She's at lunch," I left it for an hour or so then rang again. "She's still at lunch" was the reply, I thought to myself, "Two hours for lunch – either the car's broken down or I should take my sister-in-law's advice from months ago and check her out" at the same time thinking to myself surely my superstitions were wrong as things had seemed better since her return home.

I parked my telephone van up the road from Telephone House, waited, and watched. as a car pulled up right outside the Telecom building with her inside to my horror I watched as she leaned over and kissed the man in the car on the cheek, a red mist descended over me before I knew it I was running towards the car just as it was about to pull off I jumped on the bonnet catching my hand cutting it badly on a windscreen wiper, my adrenalin sky-high I felt no pain, with my wounded hand I punched the face of the man in the car as many times as I could until he screamed in pain, I stopped hitting him when he cried out even though when I had asked for the affair with my wife to finish he had not stopped or cared for my pain, which was deep in my soul and would last much longer than his superficial hurt.

As he fled, leaving the love of his life to my mercy.

I then turned my attention towards what I, unfortunately, have to call my wife.

She was standing there like a statue frozen in time, I was distraught and didn't know what to say to her or what to do, In a flash with the hand that was bleeding I rubbed my blood all over her face and hair, the next thing I knew an old man who was standing at the bus stop grabbed me by the arm and said "Stop you should never hit a woman.

By this time, I felt very weak. I just looked at him and said" I know and I haven't and I never have" I then told him "You just don't understand."

Linda had disappeared into the Telecom building which I was then taken into; a staff member bandaged my still bleeding hand, as I sat there in total shock I couldn't even speak, then within minutes two police officers were standing in front of me and about to arrest me, at that moment Linda appeared and assured them I was not at fault.

She told them she had not been attacked as people thought when seeing her covered in blood, and it was all her fault, with this information the police left and I went home.

At home, I sat with Justin watching TV telling him I had hurt my hand at work. I was so shocked and hurt it felt just like I was back on those tenement steps cold and alone only this time I was a man with my son beside me.

I didn't know what to think or what to do. I was totally confused, yet as I sat and thought I realised her worry at the time of the police being in her office was more to do with saving her and her man friend's jobs other than any concern for me.

As I sat there, I heard her key in the door she'd turned up with a friend from work too scared to be on her own although throughout over sixteen years together I had never harmed a hair on her head, as she entered the room she crawled across the floor to where I was sitting begging forgiveness with tears in her eyes.

I just sat there saying nothing. I felt lost. I could not compete with lying and cheating. It wasn't in my make-up my childhood demons were summoned up once again battering what little confidence I had and draining my energy.

I knew from my time with May some people could be very devious, but I didn't think lightning could strike me twice, although these actions differed, they were running a close second to May.

How she could be so unfaithful especially as she had a comfortable life with love showered on her from me and her son made her actions far beyond my knowledge I have to say I had worshipped the ground she walked on, every penny I earned was hers, perhaps my mistake because it left me unable to take her out or plan a surprise present leaving her in control of whatever we did, my innocence was seen as weakness, she took my kindness and used it to her advantage, taking me for granted many times and not seeing me as someone who cared for her.

All I wanted to do was to look after my family before thinking of myself; I was doing right but was so naïve.

It's hard not to sound bitter but in telling the truth in all the events of my story I have no choice it's how the cookie crumbles so to speak, my words are of my life story not to protect other people's reputations.

I believe there's no harm in telling the truth while at the same time not being too personal to the other party with so much more, I could say I save her some embarrassment while thinking of the feelings of our son, something she never did during our marriage.

As the mother of my son, I am afraid to say she was a person who loved the attention of men, and after being found out cheating again that special attention she had always received from me was gone never returning, I'm pretty sure she did not like the thought of this so made up her mind to go all out and choose another path in her life regardless of mine or our son's feelings.

Some six months later while Justin was at school and me at work, she left us each a note, both notes I still have after many years not for any sentimental reasons only for the fact they were left in an old suitcase stored in the loft which I accidentally stumbled on, and quote word for word as she wrote.

My dear Robert this is the hardest letter I have ever had to write. I am sure that if you think about it my leaving will be best for you in the end and for me. I have not been much of a wife to you but I have finally gained the courage to do what I should have done long ago, I am truly sorry for all the pain and misery that I have caused you and hope that with time you will find the happiness that you deserve and that I cannot give you. Thank you for standing by me in everything over the years. It has been appreciated. Look after Justin; he's your friend as well as your son, and look after Pooh the dog.

I will need to speak to you about the rest of my things at some time. I will ring you tonight to speak to Justin. Justin said he is going out to dig that garden at 4.15 and won't be home till later. I'll always think of you with love. Linda, PS although reading this may seem that it has been easy for me, I can only say that I Have done a lot of soul-searching and it is the most painful I have ever had to face in my life. Pooh's dinner is in the oven.

Justin's note read, My darling Justin. I am sorry that I could not tell you I was leaving. It would have been too difficult for me. I hope that you will forgive me. I do love you and always will.

Please look after Dad for me and help him and be his friend. Also, look after Pooh, make sure he gets fed. I will ring you tonight but if you want to ring me, I'm at Jan's. Please try and stay in until Dad comes home from work. Please forgive me. All my love to you. Mum.

I later learned once again from my sister-in-law, she had been having this affair for over two years, and the only reason she'd not left sooner was that the man in question had twin sons, and would not leave his wife until his sons had completed their education. I thought "Plans were being made without consideration for my son. There was never any ball and chain attached to her, in the seventeen years we had been together she had enjoyed a good life if she wanted out of her marriage I was not going to stand in her way, I would be the last to stand in the way of anyone's happiness even as in this case knowing I would be the one to carry the hurt.

During our marriage we had never argued and I had cared for her as much as possible, all of her foul moods and insults towards me were designed to ease her conscience and justify her actions, it was obvious she felt she had married too young, and from the seeds planted in her head by her father felt she had married below her class.

If only she would have given me the smallest of conversation as to what her problem was with me it may have eased some of the pain I was feeling, whatever her reasons I think Justin, and I deserved a little better than a goodbye note.

I must add my past life of losing my mother, and the poor childhood I had endured was never a reason for her to stay with me.

For example, out of any sympathy, my life's past was only touched on, never really fully spoken of with her, or her family.

In heated exchanges during our break up one of her comments was that she had picked me up from out of the gutter, in some ways true as is obvious from the start of my life in England, what she failed to remember, I had built her up to what she'd become confident, and believing in her beauty, so much so I think she thought I was not up to the standard of life she wanted to achieve.

There are only my thoughts, but very truthful. The last time I ever spoke to her I asked her "What about our son Justin?" She replied "I can have another one" I felt sorry for her knowing she would one day remember her words, and feel ashamed.

I now knew I did not know this person anymore, as a mother surely her words were not meant they were just to hurt me a little more, and to further justify her guilt, only she knows?

As for my feelings she had left me with a deep scar which has slowly healed, yet always for various reasons has left me puzzled to understand her behaviour in putting herself before her son many times, and her uncalled-for bitterness towards me, which was not reflected in her note.

I was now left to go it alone with a heavy mortgage with no contribution from my wife in what had been a shared financial arrangement.

I felt so let down by her, even though it was hard going with all the bills flooding in I couldn't bring myself to speak to her about the situation she had put me in.

As for her, I think she was so engulfed in her new life she forgot her responsibilities. I polished up on my cooking skills, and my son and I grew to rely on one another and to get by from day today.

The only problem now that his mother was gone was his school attendance suffered and as I was forced to work longer hours to make ends meet unable to keep full control over his movements.

Luckily, he was a good lad and after a few words from me, he started to toe the line and grow up fast.

We were now not just father and son, we were also best mates. Often, I would feel the hurt of my wife's leaving and feel quite lonely. I knew my son felt for me whilst dealing with his sorrow over the breakup of his happy home.

Every song I listened to on the radio seemed to in the lyrics relate to broken marriages, and broken hearts, it was obvious from the songs that so many people had suffered sad breakups from their loved ones, theirs, and my hurt played out in the words.

The songs never really eased the pain I felt.

My feelings are not needed to be described to all who have suffered heartbreak in this way but believe me, it's a terrible pain, a pain never felt by the unfaithful.

I also lost contact with my wife's family with whom I had over sixteen years built a good relationship, their support had vanished, it was as if to them I never existed, it was the classic case of blood before water.

Within days, my wife and her partner were living in what was my mother and father-in-law's home. I felt abandoned and humiliated and each day there was a feeling of sickness in the pit of my stomach.

Even the girl Cathy from Manchester who I had spent that special moment with when my son was born, spoke to me saying "Linda was happy" and that her new man "really cared for her". I was hurt and surprised at Cathy's words because she spoke to me as if I had no feelings, which if she had remembered back 16 years to when my son was born, she surely would have been better off saying nothing.

My confidence was shattered once again by her words. I had tried my best to hold my family together over many years, I knew my wife would never come back. She had done too much damage to her own, and another woman's family. This time I decided even if she remotely tried to re-enter my life there would be no chance.

I removed all her clothes from our family home and took them to her parents she rang in surprise at my actions, my only words to her with a heavy heart were to say "goodbye and good luck", I wasn't' going to make our break up into a huge drama dragging it on and on making her feel the centre of attraction as in the past, with no choice left I started divorce proceedings, we had made our beds, and now had to lie in them, she happier than me in how our marriage had ended for sure.

Though she may have thought she had dumped me, in truth I had long before lost faith in her and was clinging on for my son, and security, security I had only briefly known when with my mother.

As time would pass one thing for sure I would not have to worry about nightmares over the marriage breakup, my conscience was clear, I had tried my best if she didn't know me by now, she never would.

She had made me so happy when I had met her, but now I felt sad that she put someone before her child.

I was now thirty-seven years old and had been running uphill for thirty years. I had slipped back a few times but I wasn't going to stop running, I couldn't I had Justin to think of.

Justin was seventeen years old when Linda offered to buy me out of the house with her new partner.

I knew she was being shrewd in her first low offer and felt sure she would offer a bit more, also I knew she couldn't get another mortgage as she was tied into a mortgage with me, with no point in dragging it out I accepted her second offer.

I wasn't and never will be materialistic. The house had lost its purpose for family and happiness and now meant nothing to me, I knew with the money from her I could secure a roof over my son's and my head – although not in over-priced London.

I contacted the welfare officer for British Telecom for advice and due to the circumstances of adultery that had taken place amongst its senior staff, my wife in the department that paid me, and a strong chance of bumping into her newest man friend I was offered a transfer from the embarrassing situation I had been left in.

The welfare officers' offer rushed my thinking which at that time was so confusing.

I discussed it with my son and explained that with the money offered we could set up a home near to my brother Mitch in Liverpool in a house we could afford as in London a single wage would not secure a mortgage with other living costs on top.

I did check out the housing in Trowbridge near Danny but like London, the property prices there were out of my reach.

Divorce

It took over a year for the divorce and settlement to go through during that time while I searched for a new home in Liverpool.

Justin stayed in the x marital house and I made the 200-mile journey from Liverpool to London each weekend to be with him when my house was signed over to my x wife, I had to rely on a friend named Paul Hawkins.

Paul had an empty house for sale, he told me I could stay at any time I needed until it was sold. He was a good friend who I had not known for long.

I had built up a friendship with him through playing football, many times while I was away from Justin I could rely on Paul and his wife to watch over Justin, and if ever a saying was true it was the one that states a friend in need is a friend indeed.

Paul certainly lived up to that saying.

When back in Liverpool I was put up by my brother Mitch in the area of Walton.

While staying with him I could tell he was worried for me and at the same time, I felt I was putting a burden on him and his family.

Forever being made redundant he had several jobs since being married, it seemed the more he tried to get up the ladder of life the harder someone was kicking that ladder away.

During my time of staying with him, he was working a tough job for little money in a factory spraying steel drums, no matter how tough I knew he would never give up trying to improve his family's life.

Every weekend for over two years I travelled from my brother's house in Liverpool to London to be with my son, many times taking sick leave to prolong our time together.

I had bought an old Volvo from a workmate for the bargain price of £100; it was a tatty car yet very reliable and made the 400-mile round trip from Liverpool to London each weekend with ease, apart from one memorable time.

It was on one return journey to Liverpool with four hours of nothing to do but drive that my mind was filled with worries for Justin, and what I felt about myself, with flashes of what happened in Canada entering my mind, the life with evil May, and my dad's failures, all were now hitting me like a ton of bricks, every bit of confidence I had tried to build over the years was draining away.

As I drove along, I felt small and useless. I was at my lowest ebb.

Just then on the darkest part of the M6 motorway I had a tire blow out, I pulled the car over to the lay-by on a bend wider than the normal hard shoulder.

I got out of the car and looked at the tire as flat as a pancake and realised I didn't have a breakdown cover.

I just stood there feeling like a child. tears welled up in my eyes, I felt completely lost, I thought "Right here in this spot is where I'm going to stay" I couldn't move I honestly thought I was going to die, a feeling no mother's child should ever endure.

I just felt I couldn't take anymore, and I wondered what had I done to anybody to deserve this nightmare of a life, everything seemed to flood into my mind right back to a boy sent from all I had known.

I had done all that I could for others always feeling humble, running messages whenever asked by my aunt, submitting to May, and due to her terrified of my father wondering where my father's love had gone, then a lifetime of boosting Linda's morale trusting in her countless times only to be let down time and time again, living under stress for over sixteen years with her, and at the same time worrying over Justin and my brothers feeling I was a failure heading back to walking the streets.

All these thoughts were hitting me like a ton of bricks only now after all these years I was at that moment realising apart from my brothers I had never received any real sincere love from anyone since my mother's death, I had needed the simplest thing in life to love and to give love, and had been too eager and vulnerable in my marriage, and in all aspects of life, I had been putting other people high on a pedestal they far from deserved.

As all this battered through my head for the first time in my life I felt sorry for myself, and at that moment so alone with a feeling of total anguish I wished I could have just one big hug from someone sincere, as I looked at the wheel on the Volvo I felt as totally deflated as that tire, with that thought, I looked to the sky and for the first time in my life with a feeling of hurt from deep in my soul called out to my Mother.

Then as God is my judge a voice in my head said in sort of slow-motion "Robert, you have changed flat tires loads of times", "open the boot take the spare out", "Jack the car, change the wheel" I did exactly as I was told, that small act of changing the tire pulled me through my darkest moment, I had done something for myself, just for me I knew I was going to have to start from near the bottom again, but at least I was now a man, not a child and had a fighting chance, I realised I would have to wipe the slate clean and start believing I was somebody, and my purpose was Justin, and I could not let him down.

As I drove on, I kept asking myself over and over was my mind playing tricks "What was that all about? How could I have got into that state?" I also realised that strange night there was more to life than meets the eye, I felt I had been spiritually helped on that stretch of road, not just to keep on driving, but to keep on living.

Mentally I fought on, and for well over a year I was back and forth from Liverpool to London, time seemed to pass quickly, my son Justin was now seventeen he'd met a girl named Bridgett and rented a flat in London, He had started work as a post boy within Telecom, a job he had got through pressure I had put on his Mother to have a word with some of the top dogs she knew within Telecom.

Now with Bridgett he decided to stay in London I did not want to hurt his feelings over his choice, but It was a shock to me because now I was transferred it meant I had no way back unless I gave up my job which wouldn't have made any sense, the main thing for me was that he was happy, although I did not tell him, I was gutted at his decision and also left wondering if I had made a big mistake by leaving London.

Very pleasing and what put my mind at rest was the relationship Justin and Bridgett had they seemed to get on well together, I used to admire their relationship and thought to myself they were a perfect match for one another, although as you may have gathered I am not the best judge when it comes to relationships, Justin always made her laugh, and everything with the two of them seemed to be about having fun, something I have found to be rare in most of the couples I have known.

I was given a big surprise one day when they told me they were going to get married and even more surprised that they wanted to marry in Liverpool, they told me every time they visited me in Liverpool people my brother Mitch and I introduced them to cousin's aunts and friends were so good to them they felt sure it was where they wanted to marry. I couldn't argue – if they wanted to marry in Liverpool then Liverpool it would be.

Now instead of me going back and forth from Liverpool to London, it was Justin and Bridgett who had that task whilst planning their future.

Every weekend theirs, and my time was taken up sorting out where the reception would be held, arranging hotels where family and friends from London would be staying, etc. Bridgett was having her wedding dress made in Liverpool, and was constantly having fittings; it was also a busy time for all the main male guests from Liverpool who had to be fitted with top hats, and tails.

Most importantly for Justin and Bridgett was attending their rehearsals at Walton Church, the church they had chosen for their big day, a beautiful large sandstone building over a thousand years old.

As the wedding drew near Justin arranged to have his stag night in Liverpool a week before the big day. This would mean a first-time visit to Liverpool for his mates and Bridgett's family from London.

The stag night went down a treat with all the Londoners and Scousers mixing and having loads of banter with each other, the Londoners couldn't believe how cheap the taxis and beer were compared to London.

Bridgett's dad who I can only describe as looking like a Toby jug could not stop telling me how pleased he was his daughter was marrying my son, commenting that he was a credit to me, I knew he was right, and in my son, his daughter was marrying a good person and so constantly assured his daughter was in safe hands.

The day of the wedding couldn't have been better. The sun was shining and it was nice and warm, a perfect day for a wedding.

My thoughts as I stood with Justin listening to the sweet sound of the bells outside the church was of how handsome he looked, also I was so proud of the friendly humorous person he had become and grateful he had shown his love for me by arranging his future life with his dad in Liverpool.

To save my feelings he hadn't invited his mother to his wedding he knew the hurt I felt and the deep scar she had left me, He knew I was torn between bitterness love and sadness and didn't know how I would have reacted had she turned up, so made his decision along with Bridgett to side with me.

Later I heard she was very upset not being at her son's wedding, and although I understood her feelings it was just as upsetting for me watching Justin take his vows alone, and deep down although he kept it to himself a sad decision for Justin to have made.

I have based my life on the belief of what you do in life you will one day be answerable to a higher judgement, which one day we all have to face, although it's hard to live up to that statement I have tried, I didn't revel in her anguish, but at this moment in time, my marriage break up was too raw for any forgiveness.

After the wedding, Justin and Bridget returned to London as a happily married couple.

I visited both of them as many times as I could for over ten years of their marriage. What I observed was a really happy marriage.

The only problem was they both wanted to have children cruelly. It was found out after they had tried for some years Justin had a low sperm count, but thankfully with the help of modern science, the good news was there should be no reason why he couldn't become a dad.

On three separate occasions during their marriage, they paid £3000 for the chance of having a baby, sadly three times the attempt failed. I was a father who had not experienced this situation I could only pray God willing my son would become a father, I knew given the chance he'd be a great dad from the man I had watched him become, and without any doubt knew with his good nature he deserved to be, sadly it was out of my hands.

As time passed on just one ordinary day my phone rang. "Hello," I said. "Hi Dad," Justin answered. "Hello Justin, how are you son?" "Not too good, Dad – Bridgett's left me." "What? You're joking!" I replied I couldn't believe what I was hearing. Justin went on to say over the last few months he and Bridgett had been visiting his twin cousin Sharon who was pregnant.

When she gave birth, Bridgett was with her and since then had been very moody, and had been throwing insults at him over his not being able to father a child, as he spoke, I could sense the hurt in his voice and knew it was a serious situation, and that Bridgett was not what I had imagined.

I knew from my marriage break-up the emptiness he was feeling; I also knew what was happening to him was far worse than it had been for me. I still had him to ease my pain when my wife left.

Justin was on his own with me 200 miles away. His breakup came suddenly out of nowhere. It was fast, cold, blunt, and cruel. I immediately set off to London to be with him.

As I now had more commitments in Liverpool I was back and forth once again to support my son. He told me Bridgett was determined to become pregnant, and had met a boy in Tesco's supermarket where she worked.

This news was, yet another hard blow for him to take, and a shock to me, all I could do was pray for him, and help pull him through this sad period.

At the time he also received some support from his mother. I wondered what advice she could give. He told me that his mum had commented to him "How could she do this to you the bitch!" I thought she had forgotten what she had done to me and recalled the saying people in glass houses shouldn't throw stones, but at least she had shown some concern for her son which in the future they could build upon.
Her support was none of my business so I dealt with him my way knowing from experience what support he would need.
When not in London I would speak on the phone with him every day to rebuild his confidence, and day by day, and over the months he started to recover his strength of character and humour.
He began to tell me of a stunning girl he had met at work he told me "All the lads in work think she's top draw," and he was hoping she might take an interest in him. He had heard she was a divorcé who had a young daughter, for weeks during our conversations he kept mentioning this girl Sam.
I encouraged his feelings about her then, at last, he told me he was taking her on a date. I had no fear for him on his date, I knew his personality would shine through, and it wouldn't be just a short relationship, things were going to work out fine, and as I predicted from the very start Justin Sam, and her daughter Lauren became a solid unit.
In Sam Justin had met someone who through no fault of her own was a single mother, she was a person with a good heart, and extremely attractive.
On hearing of Justin's past marriage and the reasons for its break-up, after a short time together, and both very much in love, Sam told Justin, "I will try for a baby with you" Justin's and, my prayers were answered and thanks to Samantha on, 1st March 2004 my grandson Lewis Paul Joshua Turley one of God's miracles was born.
One lesson learned from my marriage to Linda, and knowing Bridgett both attractive was that beauty is only skin deep.

MEETING PINA

I did not think I would ever meet anyone to match my x wife's looks, yet surprisingly I did. I eventually met a naturally pretty Italian girl named Pina. She was born in London to Italian parents.

I was attending a Telecom function with some of my workmates on one of my constant returns to London when we met.

She was twenty-five years old, 5ft 2 slim and curvy with jet-black hair – everything about her attracted me, her looks, her figure, and as I got to know her honesty shone through, and importantly, she was single.

It was important to me her being single because now that I was single several women with whom I had certainly had a chance to strike up a relationship were married with children.

This included a pretty blonde woman who was almost in looks a double to my x wife. She worked in a supermarket in Edmonton where I would regularly go to get mine and Justin's weekly shopping, as I got to know her, she made it particularly clear she was interested in me.

On one of my regular visits to her till she told me outright she liked me and she had been lying on her bed one night after having a bath naked thinking of me! It was a strange feeling having just been dumped without care to then suddenly having someone else interested in me, at that moment I just thought to myself "Isn't life strange"? I didn't know what to say to her. I was so stunned; all I could say was "See you again next week. "

The next day I told a few of my workmates a little of what had occurred? They said I should get in there when I told them she was married with kids and I didn't want to cause someone else the hurt I had suffered. Their response was "You were dumped on from a great height, so why worry about someone else?" Although I was tempted by their words, and without sounding like a goody-two-shoes, my short answer to them was "No, I'm sorry I just can't do it."

I felt perhaps in their lives it seemed OK more to the point they couldn't have understood, or have suffered the pain such actions cause, although not a churchgoer I fully understood why adultery was one of the Bible's Ten Commandments, I was left with my thoughts about the whole situation which were this lady's need for attention and her forthright manner was one day going to hurt her children and husband, but it wouldn't be with me.

With Pina I wasn't breaking any rules or hearts, she was twenty-five years old and single which made her perfect for me.

During a fairly long courtship she certainly stopped me thinking there was anything wrong with me which my x wife had led me to believe, the only problem that occurred during our early relationship was as if she arrived home late after an evening out, her parents being very strict Italians would give her a relentless ear-bashing which would go on for days.

This was made worse when they discovered her late nights were due to me and made even worse when they learned I had been married and divorced with a son. At first, I would joke with Pina about the situation referring to the Godfather film when the boyfriend woke up with the horses head in his bed but soon realized it was no joke and it was my duty to go to see her mother tell her I was genuine, and my marriage break up was not my fault, my goal was to stop the mental torture she and her husband were putting their daughter through.

The day I met her mother she sat me down in her front room and listened to what I had to say about my honourable intentions towards her daughter, she was very nice to me and nodded her head as I spoke in what I thought was an approving way, I said all I could say to ease her mind, and left feeling my best done, all the time thinking I had far more problems than she would ever know all around me, and hoped If she would just give me the chance to prove to her worries for her daughter although genuine, were not well-founded.

My efforts with her mother were fruitless; she decided not to give me a chance, rejected by my wife, and now rejected for having been married was not good for my self-esteem.

This decision by her parents only forced Pina into wanting to leave home which now meant I had her putting pressure on me to ease the torment she was receiving from her mum and dad and to make our relationship more permanent.

It was a situation I could have done without, back and forth up the motorway working for telecom in a different environment worrying about Justin still getting over a broken marriage, and looking for a house left me with my head spinning.

I laid it on the line to Pina: “I'm going to be living in Liverpool. It's different from London and you will be away from all you know, what do you want to do?” She said she loved me and didn’t care where we lived, she just wanted to be with me, I had to decide to take her away, or end the relationship.

I felt she was a person who had come into my life and was too good to let go, so Needless to say Pina came with me to Liverpool and we set up home in a house on the outskirts of Liverpool, in an area called Whiston.

For over a year there was no contact from Pina's mother or father, only her brother Billy, and sister Sabatini kept in touch, a sad time for Pina. When I decided to marry Pina her mother's attitude changed immediately, I was now accepted as part of the family. I now have an extended family in Italy, and Sabatini, and Lello whenever I visit Italy a warm welcome is always assured.

From being without food so many times as a kid, I had now been introduced to the wonderful food of Italy, never dreamt of during the hungry years under May's wicked control.

One memorable time my brother-in-law took me on an Italian stag night with twenty-five of his Italian friends. I ended up in a fish restaurant at the top of a beautiful cobbled street in Amalfi. In the restaurant plate after plate of different varieties of fish were put in front of me until I thought I would burst.

At the end of the night leaving the restaurant I looked up at the stars and couldn't believe I was there. I felt so lucky it was such a beautiful place.

One thing I have learned in life is to never take anything for granted so I took that moment under the stars for all it was worth and embedded it in my mind.

My new marriage produced two lovely children, a second Son Kevin Russell named after my brothers who had died in the house fire and a beautiful daughter, named Carly.

The marriage also gave Justin a brother and sister which I had always wanted him to have and knew he desired.

To his credit never has he shown any jealousy at being in some respects pushed aside by me in bringing up another family but in many ways, I feel I let him down by leaving London even though at the time under great duress it's a cross I have to bear.

In Pina, I have discovered what a wonderful mother means to their children's development.

My children I'm proud to say have done well. Kevin and Carly are both graduates from John Moores University and on their way to successful careers.

Kevin is now a surveyor and Carly is one step away from becoming a solicitor, or health worker she can't make up her mind, but I think health worker.

Both have found nice partners in Stacey and Jaz. Kevin is soon to be a dad of a boy he will name Joseph Robert Turley, giving me a second grandchild, due on the 11. 1. 2013. And now Carly has married and is about to give birth to a boy, Reuben Dhillon due on 6. 6. 15.

Also, I have received the great news that Kevin and Stacey are soon to have a brother for Joey and are to name him Vincent.

After working hard from the start of his career in British telecom Justin moved jobs and is now a manager with a large company, and very happy with Sam.

Sam has proved to be a wonderful wife, and mother, and I am now also a proud grandfather of Lewis Turley, he is the apple of my eye making me so happy, and is, after all, what life is all about.

Pina's family Living in London is ideal for me although it's 200 miles from Liverpool visiting them means I can have constant extra meetings with Justin his partner Sam grandson Lewis and Lauren, with my new family joining in

Still, after all, I've strived for, I have a problem with some jealousy with my second wife with regards to Justin.

This is a subject I battled with every day and won.

Deserted

God works in a mysterious way. Both my brothers regarding their marriages suffered the same fate as me, perhaps the three women who became our wives were there for us in a time of need, and not for our future, and perhaps we have been put to a test in this life?

My Brother Mitch was left with his children by his wife when his son Michael was seven, and his daughter Vicky eleven.

Mitch is the most fantastic father any child could wish to have. I watched him with admiration over the years during his marriage when bringing up his kids, and whilst on his own.

When I say my brothers and I were on our own with our children I mean it, there was no one to fall back on, Unfortunately, we all lived 200 miles apart in London, Liverpool, and Trowbridge.

Mitch made some mistakes along the way as did Danny and I, although nothing serious, and we all ended up with well-balanced young people in our lives.

I taught myself many skills like plumbing, woodwork car maintenance etc and went to college gaining a certificate in electronics.

Danny stood as a Labour councillor in his new hometown of Trowbridge. Mitch now works with British Telecom and was the main source of documentation gathering for this story.

Small achievements within the great scheme of things, but massive to us yet, always leaving us with the unanswered question of what we may have achieved had life been a little kinder.

Strange, but true all three brothers, when together for short periods detected jealousy from our wives due to our closeness, it was like there was a force working against us, desperate to keep us apart.

Neither Danny nor Mitch remarried, forgiving their wives countless times took its toll on them both, sadly to never trust in marriage.

All three brothers have had no luck in the women we've met, but one day we will once again meet the woman who means so much, our mother.

Mitch's beautiful daughter Vicky married, and he is the proud grandfather of two polite little boys' Cameron and Kyle who always look forward to weekend visits. Sadly, on my brother Mitch's ex-wife's side of the family the horrendous genetic disorder Huntington's prevails.

Vicky underwent predictive testing for the faulty gene regrettably the result came back positive to prevent passing this terrible disease to her unborn children genetic embryonic procedures were carried out successfully on two embryos allowing her two healthy sons and we all pray for any breakthrough in medical science that will help Vicky and other sufferers of this dreadful condition.

Danny's wife left him when his children were twelve and fifteen years old. He struggled with no support but cared for them bringing them up to be fine young adults.

His son Daniel attended Hull University and is on his way in life.

His daughter Eleanor is still studying hard at college, and I'm sure will be successful in her life.

I have often asked myself how three brothers who had every obstacle to overcome suffering, loss hurt, and betrayal ended up the people we never became selfish, putting everything we earned on the table showing complete love to our wives, and children.

My conclusion was locked deep in our minds was the knowledge we had gained through our great loss, and in surviving life's uphill battle that love, honesty, and home life was the number one priority.

It was a testament to the love our mother gave in the short time she was with us that as men, we could hold our heads up our honesty let 3 wives and mothers leave their responsibilities

More than most, we knew the importance of good parents and had tried our best in marriage, each of our wives left us not because we were not good people but it seemed for a better financial position.

Mitch along with his children was deserted for a night school teacher, Danny for an old university friend of his wife who'd climbed the ladder to a well-paid job, and me for a much better-paid supervisor, perhaps our lack of need for the material things in life and the effects of our trauma leaving us unassertive had been our downfall regarding our marriage, we had put all our efforts into providing well for the family never asking much of our loved ones, never craving the better car fancy clothes or expensive meals out, to explain burnt to a cinder every stitch of anything we owned, special toys mementos material things lost forever on that one night in 1957, that today would have meant so much, and yet mean nothing compared to losing a family life and the love and care we shared so briefly, hence our lack of need for things and more for the need of love, and to give love.

All that had been thrown at us we had overcome, and we could never leave our children to anything like a similar fate to ours, even the thought of it would have felt like a dreadful failure.

Return to Canada

One of our children presented a gift of unbelievable kindness to Danny Mitch and, I It was a couple of weeks before Christmas in 2001 when I answered the phone to Mitch's daughter Vicky, as I picked the phone up, I heard. "Hi Rob", Vicky went on, "I've bought something for dad this Christmas and I would like you and Danny to share in it.

"She went on to say "Over the years my dad has always kept and now and again looked over pictures and little bits of memorabilia from Canada", I have always felt so sad for him over the years", "so Graham and I" have decided to hold back from buying a house for a little longer and have bought you my dad and Danny tickets to return to Canada in April 2002" "Rob"? "Rob"? "Rob", "are you there"? I was there but I could not speak. My throat had closed and I was choked. It had been forty-four years since that dreadful night and its memory, Oh my God Canada? The Name sent feelings of love and fear flashing into my mind. In my next thought I was worrying what might lie ahead, after a long pause I thanked Vicky in what she must have felt was a low-key way, she must have thought I was ungrateful, but I couldn't help my reaction. I was stunned.

All of life's obstacles surviving gaining the necessity of a roof over our heads marrying divorcing looking after our kids and trying to make ends meet meant returning to Canada hadn't been something we could think about or hope to achieve, having said all that the main factor was that there could never be a return to Canada unless as three brothers who left together, we returned all three together.

In over forty years this hadn't been dreamt of or spoken about while we were stuck in our bubbles of everyday life.

Vicky worked for the government dealing in the birth, and death certificate department in Southport Merseyside, in the office being around Christmas time talk was about what presents to get for various relations all the staff seemingly feeding off each other for good ideas on what to buy their loved ones, during these conversations Vicky told them of the surprise she had planned for her dad and uncles when quizzed as to why such a gift by some workmates, she told them the reasons behind her gesture, some of the ladies were in tears at the wonderful gift.

A group of staff members felt so strongly about our story they decided to ring the Liverpool Echo newspaper and tell a reporter about our surprise trip to our past.
The newspaper took a strong interest in our story and interviewed us about our emotional return to Canada. One lady from the paper said to my brother Michael "what an amazing story I can't wait to go home and hug my kids, and to one day tell them of your sad story.
They wrote a nice article with "Pilgrimage to a Tragic Past" as the headline, the echo newspaper then informed the BBC who also took an interest in our story and televised a short film about our journey back to Canada, the news item was helped by my brother Mitch with the filmed news article of our arrival in England way back in 1958 which he had obtained from BBC archives some years earlier.
This early film was incorporated which made our trip more interesting. A gentleman from the BBC named Rob Cave requested of us to inform the BBC on our return from Canada so that a follow-up program could be aired regarding what discoveries we might make in Montreal, we agreed and felt a little bit special that after all the years that had pasted a small part our life, and sorrow was to be acknowledged in this way.
Before our journey, we commissioned a stonemason to inscribe a small marble plaque with the words "Mum, Russell, and Kevin" with the words. "SADLY, MISSED We were left with little information – only knowing our loved ones were in a plot donated by the Bishop of Montreal.
What this meant we didn't know we had the name of the cemetery Hawthorn Dale, and a few old pictures of us as children with a house in the background, a house we had always wondered who may have lived there or even if it may have been the house we had lived in, we now hoped to find out.
The day before leaving we received a phone call from the BBC, they informed us that Canadian television wanted to interview us when we arrived and if it was ok by us to grant the interview, we all willingly agreed to their request.

The day we left our emotions were all over the place one minute it felt like we were going to meet someone we loved, and had not seen for years giving an excited feeling in the pit of our stomachs, the next minute reality hit home on what we were about to embark upon, and we knew we were on a journey to perform a long-lost duty which was to pay our respects to loved ones.

How we would feel when we arrived, and what we would achieve when our search was over, we had no real idea, we were leaving blind on just a hope, and a prayer.

It was at this time our father's memories had they been shared with us would have been so important, and a great help sadly that wasn't to be.

Mitch's daughter Vicky, and partner Graham kindly took us to Manchester airport. They wished us luck and we were on our way to a search for a lost childhood and unanswered questions.

The journey to get to Montreal must have been one of the longest ever. The travel agent Vicky booked our journey which sent us via several different connections instead of a direct flight; we left from Manchester Airport, and first flew into Charles De Gaulle.

After a three-hour wait, we boarded our flight across the Atlantic arriving in Boston USA, it was just after the horror of 9/11 when we arrived in Boston, and security was tight.

On the entry form at the border control Danny and I were told three times to get our date of birth right before being allowed in – we kept on putting the day then the month and year which is not how they do it in America, they put month day and year on their forms, the border guard checking us was no help, he just kept sending us back to do it again, never explaining where we were going wrong, we were getting annoyed with him, on the third time of trying had it been wrong again I think we would have ended up in jail, but third time lucky Danny and I got the dates the way he wanted, Mitch looked on in amusement as he had a Canadian passport.

As we passed through customs to transfer to our Canadian flight an American lady checking passports commented on our being three Brothers with a sort of amazed look on her face.

Somehow, she seemed to know we were different from most that passed her way that day, I felt we were radiating a glow something spiritual which though unexplainable it was all around us, it was as if what we were doing was written and meant to be, and the nearer we came to our goal the more it must have shown.

After another long wait at Boston airport, we finally boarded a small 50 seat aeroplane for the final part of our journey to Montreal. After a flight of just over an hour, we were informed to fasten our seat belts, looking down as we approached to land, all the lights in Montreal were sparkling, reminding me of Christmas. I commented "It's like the tinsel town" just for a moment. I was seven years old again.

We had been travelling for over sixteen hours. I remember saying to my brothers "Nothing's ever easy for us, is it?" They smiled and acknowledged my words with a nod of their heads.

The three of us knew we had seven days with no time to spare to find our past and it would be very emotional so much so we couldn't wait to land and place our feet on the land that was our spiritual home and to begin our quest.

When we reached our hotel we found the receptionist spoke French which we were not expecting, as he spoke to us we stared at him scratching our heads until he realised we did not understand one word he was saying, then in broken English he explained how much we needed to pay for our room, on paying he showed us to a large room with three single beds, as we were shattered from our long journey we were very tempted to just get into the comfy looking beds and sleep.

We were now in a different time zone and our body clocks were out of sync back in England it was midnight in Montreal five hours behind, it was only seven in the evening. Exhausted as we were, we had all noticed the hotel bar so decided on a drink before going to bed, also believing we might gather some information as to how far the cemetery and our old neighbourhood were from the hotel.

We approached the bar and ordered three beers. The barmaid said some words in French which baffled us. When she realised we did not understand she explained in English "You have to tip.

At first, we thought it was rude of her to be so upfront, but all three of us decided it was perhaps a cultural misunderstanding on our part, we now knew the rules of bar service in Montreal which was so different to England where you only tip if you want.

After our third drink and good tips, the barmaid knew we now knew the rules and smiled at us for the rest of the night.

At the bar, we spoke to an American who explained to us some of the customs of Quebec.

According to him, the French Canadians did not like to speak English for reasons going back centuries to their battles over land with an English general known as Wolfe. This information left us with the realisation it would be harder than we thought to find our past, but our spirits were high no matter what problems might occur with communications we wouldn't be deterred, nothing was going to stop the three of us from paying our long overdue respects to our loved ones.

We retired to bed knowing what lay ahead would drain us mentally we were about to put all our energy into finding information and places close to our hearts, but through circumstances of fate had not been achieved for forty-four years.

The next day we woke up at 6 am. It was a freezing morning in April. Ironically, we had left in April of 1958 and were now back in April 2002, a 44-year gap.

We decided to stroll down the road from the hotel to kill a bit of time as it was still quite dark and too early to start on our priority which was to visit Hawthorn Dale cemetery, as we walked, we saw a pile of snow and couldn't resist a snowball fight.

I realised on that cold morning we were recapturing a memory that was buried deep in our childhood memories and I couldn't help thinking how many wonderful times we had missed in our time away from Montreal.

CBC TELEVISION NEWS

We returned to the hotel feeling anxious as the time was now upon us to pay our respects. We were about to book a cab when there was a knock on the door of our hotel room.

We opened the door to see a young woman standing there with an older gentleman. "Hello, I'm Erin Boudreau, this is cameraman Jean François from Canada Now News", "we have been informed by the BBC of your story and if it's ok with you we'd like to ask a few questions whilst filming an interview with you." We agreed to their request although a little upset that our immediate plans were now on hold.

While Erin spoke to us Jean went to get his camera, on his return, he started filming, we produced pictures and spoke of what we hoped to achieve, the more we told them the more especially the cameraman wanted to know, he was an experienced news cameraman whereas Erin was quite a young reporter who followed her cameraman's lead.

After quite a long interview he informed us he was going to ring his office to request more time with us as he thought our story was of more interest than he had been led to believe by the BBC.

After a conversation with his television company they were granted more time with us, they then informed us they would like to accompany you to the cemetery to film events as they unfolded." Wow – we were over the moon.

We now had assistance to find our past and it was to be recorded. We had never been treated special. But at that moment in time, we felt very special.

After ordering us a taxi they followed us to the cemetery, once there we had microphones attached to our lapels. Jean the cameraman said he would discreetly film us from a distance as we searched for our family's grave.

After an hour of searching, we still could not locate the grave, we knew we were close because a map we had obtained of the cemetery indicated the whereabouts of each grave by their plot number.

As time went by it seemed we were not going to find what was to us the most important spot on earth, one of our main challenges was half the cemetery where the springtime sun had not reached was under a foot of snow, both Jean and Erin joined in our search but still there was no grave to be found.

Then from out of the cemetery offices appeared a couple of officials, one was a giant of a man who spoke in French to Jean the cameraman, the official explained that the Bishop of Montreal plot was an unmarked grave.

This came as a complete shock to us we had no idea it was unmarked, in fact, a pauper's grave, we felt a mother with her two babies who had died in such a tragic way could surely have been afforded a small headstone by her mother our father or a wealthy city like, Montreal.

We felt what a truly sad end it was for our loved ones, we now realised the small plaque we had brought from England was to be far more important than we had first thought, bringing them some recognition for their past lives which were so important to us.

The cemetery officials told us they would find and return with the groundsman who would be able to supply measurements and pinpoint the exact location of the grave.

As we waited for the groundsman it dawned on us without the TV people being with us, we would have had real trouble finding our loved ones' grave, because seeing a TV cameraman the staff had left their warm offices, it was our lucky day, and such is the power of TV.

As we waited a nice fellow turned up in a dumper truck and said "Hello", "I am the groundsman", he then started to carefully measure from different gravestone until finally stopping and pointing, then saying "Here is your grave" We thanked him shook his hand and asked him where he was from "I'm originally from Portugal," he said, we were so pleased he had found our mother's and brothers' grave, even from that short meeting we felt he would now always be a friend.

We also knew he had to leave but our friendship although short-lived would never be forgotten.

We then stood together on the spot he had found for us with our arms across one another's shoulder, we closed our eyes in prayer, then laid our plaque in its rightful place. Knowing we were on camera we held back our tears in a manly sort of way, we were called separately to one side by Erin "Could you describe how you feel at this moment?" she asked.

We all answered that we felt deeply sad with a knotted feeling in our stomachs, and so overwhelmed that we were finally here paying our respects, and marking their resting place.

We left the cemetery and returned to our hotel with a sense something was not right, we three brothers all agreed we needed to return to the cemetery on our own for a private moment together without cameras, and other people looking on.

Erin and Jean said they would want to finish with some more filming tomorrow, we asked them to do it the next day to which they agreed. This left us with a day to ourselves and our own time to reflect, and revisit.

The next day we returned to the cemetery with flowers and a small garden spade. We had planned to bury some more trinkets brought from people back home simple things although meaningful to all our friends in England, like a watch strap from a special friend of mine Billy Dunn which had belonged to his departed dad.

This watch strap was his treasured personal memory of his dad, but he felt in passing it to me, he was safe in the knowledge it would be in a place of love and respect for all time.

We placed the watch strap and other mementos in a small pile and secured the plaque above them, we shed our tears and took in the surroundings where our loved ones lay thinking of our father, and the many people standing in the very spot all those years broken-hearted.

One of those trinkets buried was a little duck attached to a hair bobble that had belonged to my daughter. If you pressed it would make a quacking noise.

As we stood back from the grave it was a good foot under the ground, and impossible to quack without being pressed, but I swear it quacked, I said "Did you hear that duck quack"?, "You're Quakers", "No", I said, "I heard it", I said no more, but deep down I knew my lost Brothers had acknowledged my small gift.

There was something very special happening that day, and a photograph would much later prove me right with some strange happenings in its background.

We stayed for hours until we had to leave that special place which was now firmly embedded in our memories. Now we had three days left in Canada with so much still to do, Erin and Jean turned up the following morning and took us to a private room in the hotel where they conducted a lengthy interview with the three of us, asking all about our lives back in England and our memories of the tragic night so long ago. When the interview was completed, they asked if they could accompany us back to our old neighbourhood, we gladly agreed this was like a dream come true – we knew we could achieve more with them.

Arrangements were made to pick us up the following day when they left, we were so excited like children we couldn't wait.

We now had the evening to get through what with the build-up before leaving for Canada the different time zones and the emotions we were going through. We felt tired, but we fancied a beer before bed so headed to the hotel bar.

Once there we sat down and were discussing the day's events when a woman who had been sitting near to us with two shady-looking characters decided to leave their company and uninvitedly sit herself down at our table.

She seemed a little drunk "Are you from England?" she asked. "Yes," we replied.

She went on to tell us that she had been an air stewardess and had been to England many times, the next words from her mouth were extremely foul – she started to curse the Queen: "Bloody Elizabeth", "bloody Queen!" Some of her comments were so rude I would not repeat them, we informed her although our Queen had no real alliance with royalty and didn't know what her problem was.

It was at that moment that Danny spotted the two shady characters she had been sitting with leaving and taking her handbag with them.

On seeing this Danny went straight to the barmaid to tell her what he had just witnessed, she called the foul-mouthed woman to her and told her, her handbag was stolen, all of a sudden from being a drunken abusive woman she broke into tears, "My money my house keys – what am I going to do!" If she had been just a little bit civil when she first sat with us, we would have helped by giving her a few bucks, alas because of her earlier attitude we decided although sympathetic to keep well out of her problem.

It also soon dawned on us that we had a lucky escape. Had Danny not seen her handbag taken undoubtedly the minute we had left the bar the finger of guilt would have been pointed at us resulting in police knocking on our hotel door, Just the thought of being locked up for the remainder of our trip sent shivers down our spines.

Mitch and I praised Danny for being so aware, at the same time thinking perhaps that night our overworked guardian angel was looking over us once again.

The next morning at nine o'clock Erin Boudreau and Jean arrived, this time they had a large four-by-four truck which meant we could all travel together.

Erin told us our old Neighbourhood of Mackayville was now known as La Fleche, due to Montreal's large French influence.

Once again, we thanked our lucky stars, we had their support as we would have been trying to find Mackayville which had ceased to be, forty-two years earlier in1959.

As we drove down one road my brother Mitch asked them to stop, he had noticed we were in Grand Alley the road in which he was born.

We hadn't planned for this, but it was wonderful.

Mitch was the only one of us surviving brothers born in Canada and was excited at finding his birthplace so unexpectedly.

As Jean filmed him looking for the house Danny and I realised this must have been where our mother had first set up home on her return from England.

With this new awareness, our sentimental feelings started to take hold, we could almost feel our mother's presence.

To our disappointment, the house numbered 3276 no longer existed, in-between two houses where it should have been was just an empty plot.

As we moved on not far up Grand Alley Jean turned into De Gaulle Street, as Jean drove slowly down the street each house number took us closer to our former home making my heart beat a little faster.

It was Danny who spotted our old house first "there it is – 1525. As we got out of the car we stood and stared at what was once our home, our memories had faded although we knew it was very similar to what we had locked in our memories.

Over forty years had passed with only a newspaper picture of a burnt-out shell always fresh in our minds, not the perfect house we now stared at.

Encouraged by Jean we knocked at the door of the house that was once our home.

I don't know if I was disappointed or not when there was no answer, I recall saying to my Brothers "I don't think we are meant to go back in there" my brothers nodded, all three in wonderment of what lay behind the door that was once our family home

FINDING OUR PAST.

Unfortunately, the only picture we had of us all as a complete family was taken facing away from our old house, we held up the small picture and lined it up to where we would have been standing all those years ago, and there in the background was the house, we had always wondered about still looking the same.

Which to help you understand is the house on the front cover of my book. Jean suggested we knock to see if whoever lived there had any memories of the night of the house fire, we took up his idea and knocked on the door. We were greeted by a lady who spoke French with no English vocabulary whatsoever.

As Jean filmed Erin spoke to her in French on our behalf then relayed to us that the lady was about to phone her husband who she was sure would be able to recall the night as he had lived there all his life.

After a fifteen-minute wait a gentleman slightly startled by having a news cameraman, and reporter outside his house appear, then in broken English, he said he remembered the night only vaguely as he was only ten at the time.

He did recall the bodies of the deceased being laid on his lawn, he knew his father Robert Nelson had helped to try to rescue people other than that he could not help.

As he spoke my brothers, and I moved towards the little piece of the lawn he had pointed to it was of great significance to us, and another part of our past life we now were aware of.

I watched as my brother Danny held his head in his hands. Mitch and I put our arms around him, and we stood for a minute saying a small prayer over the piece of land my mother and brothers had been placed on that dreadful night.

It was then the gentleman we now know as Ronald said as if just waking up to reality "One moment I will phone my brother He was eighteen at the time of the fire perhaps, he can help" He then spoke on his mobile phone for a short period then passed the phone to Danny who listened and when switching the phone off told us "He wants to see us now he said the man on the phone is saying, 'please, please come to my house now, I can't wait to see you. 'We were overwhelmed. Even Jean, an experienced cameraman, was amazed at the sudden turn of events.

Once again, they requested more time from their TV Company to follow the story. We left De Gaulle Street following Ronald to his brother's house, after a drive of about thirty minutes we pulled into a double-fronted driveway, there stood a huge pebble-built Canadian-looking house; we were all greeted by a smartly dressed gentleman who introduced himself as Claude.

He then stared at us and said "now let me see you must be Danny and you're Robert, and you must be Michael" he hugged us all one at a time and said "all these years I knew you would come one day" I immediately told him, "It's been a long time but we have had it a bit hard over the years" "I know you have had it hard" he said, in an unbelievable statement, "and I have prayed for you many times.

As he spoke, I remembered all those times at rock bottom when I had hoped and prayed someone must care and understand about what happened to us in Canada, well that person was now standing right in front of me, and I now knew my prayers had never been in vain. "For me," he said, "to have you three boys standing in front of me – well, to me it's a miracle." We all hugged two sets of brothers reunited through tragedy after more than forty years all with tears in our eyes remembering events of one night long past.

"Please," Claude said "I have something I want to show you, please wait "one moment." wondering what he meant we watched as he climbed the stairs.

While he was gone, we stared at his beautiful amazing home, his brother Ronald told us Claude, and his wife had built it themselves way back in 1969 from pebbles they had gathered from a stream that ran at the bottom of their property, sadly Claude's wife had passed away some years earlier.

When Claude reappeared, he beckoned us to the table saying "I have here some material" he then unwrapped from brown paper all the original newspapers from the French La Presse, Montreal-Matin, the Montreal Star, and Gazette, telling in great detail, of the tragedy that had affected in different ways each one of us.

My brothers and I were stunned as we went through the pages reading stories such as how it was though how the fire had started, which I referred to earlier in my story, most importantly we had an eye witness account in Claude of events only he could have known.

He told to us as events unfolded before his eyes on that dreadful night his saddest and most painful memory was when alongside the body of my Mother and Brothers the baby pushchair in which Kevin had died was placed, making the loss of a baby clear and so sad.

He went on to tell us how he and his father Robert Nelson had battled with my father in a vain attempt to save lives.

As he spoke this amazing jigsaw of life was filmed, by an astonished cameraman especially regarding the keeping of newspapers for 44 years, an experienced cameraman knew only too well fact was sometimes stranger than fiction.

We thanked Claude and his brother Ronald for holding these papers for so many years.

He then presented the papers to us: "Here take them, they are yours". Claude explained his mother who had passed away two months earlier was the person who had kept them safe.

When she had died everything relating to the area apart from our newspaper stories had been thrown away. Claude said he had kept only our newspapers in the hope of experiencing what had just happened.

It was a wonderful gesture from a mother, and son in memory of my mother, and amazing of them to think of my brothers and me for such a long time.

We once again thanked them, hugged, and left our addresses; never would we want to lose contact with our newfound friends.

As we drove from his house I wondered if we would have had anything like his house if fate had been kinder, but I also realised it was an unanswerable question.

Erin and Jean returned us to our hotel later that evening thanking us for sharing our story with them.

Although we would not be in Canada when they were to broadcast our story on television, they promised to send us all the footage taken.

A promise they kept. It had been an amazing four days with Erin and Jean the camera Man we had found out so much thanks to their help.

We had one more visit to make, that was to friends of my mother and father, their names were Dot and Bing Ronco.

When we arrived at Dot and Bing's house it was our last day in Montreal, the week had flown it would have been nice to have had more time with them, with the little time we did have we bombarded them with questions.

We learned our mother and father were very much in love and they took great care of us. Dot and Bing took us to the chapel where our parents were married.

They told us on the day of the funeral three days after the fire our father had to be held back by several men as he wanted to open the coffins to take one last look at his wife and children.

We also learned we never attended the funeral.

Dot then told of her disgust at our grandmother who washed her hands of us and offered no help. Dot had told her face to face she would never abandon her grandchildren under any circumstance her words to our grandmother she told us, were fruitless.

One item of information concerning our grandmother goes back to about 1974 before we knew of her failures towards us, she came to England and with the help of government offices found our address in London.

At this time she was staying with her daughter in Birmingham.

We rushed to see her, yet left not feeling any real connection – especially after she had commented perhaps our mother was better off dead the way our father had kept her having babies, after those words we just switched off from asking her questions of any meaning, feeling perhaps her contact was only due to her feelings of guilt from way back in1957.

We learned that she was fairly well off, and had married twice since the death of her first husband, our grandfather.

We were told she had visited many countries in her life and wherever she stayed for some reason she always left her shoes in that country.

On hearing this I thought of all the times my brothers and I were shoeless and how we could have done with her support, support never there.

It now seemed she was trying to ease the cross she bore by checking up on us seventeen years later when truthfully for many years we were to her forgotten grandchildren.

There was never any more contact after that meeting with our grandmother. About two years later we were informed by my mother's sister that she had passed away and she had left 1000 dollars to be shared by my brothers and me.

At that time Mitch wanted to go to Canada for the funeral but was discouraged from going. The reason he was discouraged was only known by my mother's family, as to my feelings towards my absent grandmother, I forgive her as I will never fully know her reasons for actions taken all those years ago.

We left Canada worn out, yet we had achieved all that was humanly possible. We had pieced together our past lives, and now had sad, and fond memories to look back on which meant a lot.

Danny commented it was the best week of his life, partially due to the time we had spent together as three brothers, a treasured memory during one magical week after so many losses.

On our return to England, we were contacted by BBC Television, who told us they had made a mistake covering the first part of our story too early, and due to the time lapses, they would regretfully not be revisiting it.

They then asked me if I would give a half-hour interview on Radio Merseyside which I agreed to.

Arriving for the interview I asked the receptionist to please pass on a message to the presenter Roger Philips, I wanted his first question to be “Why forty-four years till your return to Canada?”

“Well,” I said, “to live as a young child without a mother and have to fight every day of your life to survive then when reaching adulthood you have started from the bottom with forces working against your efforts makes any thoughts for yourself and your past to be put to one side, and I hope in this interview to help you and the listeners understand why 44 years,”

I answered all his questions about my past life and our trip to Canada. At the end of the interview, he commented “What an amazing story! You should write it down” I answered “I will try one day ``"you should” was his reply.

A BBC researcher must have picked up on and Passed onto the BBC network how May had soaked us with her urine.

The same disgusting storyline happened shortly after my interview in the EastEnders soap opera almost exactly as I had described it, If it shocked the viewers of East enders and made people more aware of the evil things that go on behind closed doors, and helped some small child somewhere who was living through similar, then all the more reason I'm glad to tell my story.

To our surprise we received a wonderful photograph from Claude Nelson taken from his family house back in 1950s Mackayville, revealing our house before the fire with Danny standing by our gate it was so important to us to see our house fully intact, seeing the windows so beautifully dressed a reminder of our mother's care for our home, now for all to see and leaving no one in doubt of the lady she was and how great was our loss.

In sending this photograph it proved to be another wonderful gesture from a very special family.

Also, with the picture was a hand-written note expressing their heartfelt feelings at our visit penned by Ronald Nelson who told us he rarely wrote in English. He describes his family's feelings.

His words read. The strangest thing happened yesterday. Three men, 3 brothers came into our home, with a smile on their faces and tears in their eyes, they came from far away in distance, and much further away in time. They came into the present three men from the past. Searching for a missing link in their life, knocking at our door for answers, 3 French Canadians 3 Québécois, with pictures in their head and hands, shared those sad memories with them, tried to give them a little something of what they were searching for, brought more tears to their eyes and maybe relief in their hearts,3 nice men came and went away and I didn't sleep well that night, my head filled with their sorrows and our past, what else is left to say we tried our best to help. My wife is very happy to have been there for them, we wish these brothers and the people they love all the happiness that can be lived on this earth, and a very special thank you to the lady that made their dream come to reality. Georgette Paquette Nelson., our dear mother.

Danny's passing

As I come near to the end of my story, one of the main reasons I wrote it with all its misfortune, the saddest and most upsetting part I have to write to date is that on 22nd June 2008 my brother Danny died at the age of sixty.

He was a survivor along with my brother and myself, the bond we had I can't easily put into words, what I can say is some nights before I go to sleep I want to dream about my brother and I feel so frustrated when I don't, I feel so sad I wasn't there to help him, yet I soon come back down to reality say a small prayer to ease my pain, and think positively about my time spent with him.

He had grown to be such a lovely man and was taken too early whilst on his own. His daughter had been with him just before he died and had noticed he was not looking too well, she asked him if he wanted her to stay with him rather than be picked up by her mother.

Unselfishly my brother told her not to worry and go on the day out with her mother. As the car horn sounded, she left.

He died from a heart attack on his own which for me is a painful thought as I wonder how he felt, and what his last thoughts may have been.

My hope for all when this time comes is that what flashes of your past life is what you want to see.

When told of Danny's death Mitch and I rushed to Trowbridge just to be near to where he was. When we arrived, there was an empty feeling of loss.

Over the years whenever we visited, he would always be there with a smile and a hug this time painfully it was not going to be the same.

We did not know where he lay as there was no contact between us, and his estranged wife.

At a total loss as to what to do we stopped for a cup of coffee in the town centre as we stood at the counter of the café Mitch turned one page of the local gazette which was sitting on top of the counter, amazingly at that first turn of the page staring at us was Danny's obituary along with the name of the Chapel where he was at rest.

Within minutes we were by his side – all three together for the last time, my brother Mitch and I felt Danny had led us to that coffee shop, even in death spiritually he was not going to let his brothers down.

At that moment alone with Danny our whole life was flashing in front of us and it seemed so short, I touched his hair which he must have had cut only days before his death, and smiled as he had had it spiked, and it looked so cute how I wished this moment wasn't happening.

One abiding memory of my brother Danny as I stood beside his coffin flashed into my mind which made me smile, it was when I thought of him during the time his beloved Liverpool won the famous European cup game known as "the Miracle in Istanbul" in 2005.

I had phoned him that night and I had never known him so happy and God knows he deserved that small moment of joy.

My young brother Mitch was in tears during what would be our last ever earthly sighting of our big brother.

We kissed him goodbye, and left the funeral parlour broken-hearted knowing it would be an uphill battle to get over our loss, but knew he would forever be in our thoughts and never a day would pass when he would not be spoken of by his brothers Mitch and I.

During Danny's time in Wiltshire, he had worked as a groundsman on the canals. He stood as a labour councillor without success, eventually, he had become a shop steward in Bowyers' meat factory in Trowbridge Wiltshire.

At his funeral, there were hundreds of his friends, some from the Ship Inn, his local pub, and many of his workmates from Bowyers, along with friends Billy, Les, Eugene, and Ann from Liverpool.

Six Turley family members sadly, but proudly carried his coffin – his Son Daniel brothers Mitch, and I, and his nephews Justin Michael, and Kevin. Tears fell as the song "Danny Boy" rang out during the service.

In my tribute to Danny, I wanted the mourners to hear of Danny's life, so I told it in this way. I began by thanking all who had come to pay their respects and saying how proud they had made my brother Mitch, and Danny's children feel.

I continued by saying Danny was the eldest of six brothers sadly losing his Mother and three Brothers at a young age, because of this Danny had an uphill struggle all his life.

Time and time again whenever life knocked him down, he picked himself up and was always there as a Brother he was a shoulder to lean on for all the people he knew and loved.

I continued, "Some of his friends here today have said of him, I loved him for his honesty, another said he was a real man" Feeling choked I went on "It is always sad when someone dies young Danny being just sixty.

Danny had borne so much in his life he had become through no fault of his own a survivor ageing him early, and wearing him out, but now God had seen enough and said come on Dan let me lift your worries you have been through enough you have passed my test, it's been a long time your mothers waiting, she has never left your side.

Danny had lived in many places – Montreal Canada, Liverpool London, Bath, and finally Trowbridge, a place he loved. He especially loved the people in the area. I Ended by adding "Till we meet again", "God bless my special brother Danny" My brother Mitch added a similar text whilst in tears feeling gutted.

Andy the manager of the Ship Inn pub in Trowbridge Wiltshire Danny had frequented him. He was a true friend to anybody who needed help, and would always pass on good advice.

After the service, many of his workmates approached Mitch and me with stories of how Danny had helped them at work, stories of the many times he had gone to management to fight their corner, and save their jobs.

A lady friend from Danny's work named Pat Morgan, said in a broad west country accent I loved your Danny, a simple thing to say, but wonderful to hear, all the tributes at such a sad time were extremely moving.

My brother Mitch and I now had one more very important duty to fulfil as we were now responsible for Danny's ashes.

Returning to Liverpool from Trowbridge we searched Anfield cemetery for the grave of our Brother Victor, who had died as a baby in 1948.

We located his grave thanks to a local historian named Bob Halliday, a remarkable man who has dedicated much of his time researching the cemetery that opened in1863.

We discovered our brother Victor had sadly been laid to rest in an unmarked grave along with other unfortunate children whose deaths were as a result of hard times, just after the war in 1948, a sad lonely resting place that without the historians help we would never have been able to find.

We had another plaque made with the words "Daniel George and Victor Alexander Turley" inscribed along with their dates of birth, and death, sadly so far apart in life and death.

We buried Danny's ashes with his brother Victor and added some soil we had brought back from Hawthorn Dale cemetery in Canada.

At the time when we took the soil from Montreal, we didn't know what to do with it but now realized bringing it back meant this small bit of earth in some symbolic way was bringing our family closer together and renewing a bond never to be broken.

As I close my story, although with much more I could have told, I must point out the few people who wronged us and tried to break our spirit, mercifully; many good people crossed our paths with kindness and love.

I thank my father's family, aunt Liz, aunt Mary, cousin Jean and Evelyn for their support over the three years that we were placed on their doorstep without warning during hard times.

I am thankful to all the people who told me I should write this story, added to by the spiritual feelings and occurrences which encouraged my efforts. 3 brothers although scarred by past events Thank God for our time together, and due to strange accuracies in our lives which I would try to explain If more equipped are left with the belief, there is an afterlife, a time when we will be reunited as a complete family.

If only I could turn back time touch and hold my loved ones, how wonderful it would be.

Thank you for reading my story I hope whoever reads it may gain some knowledge from it, in that if or whenever life gets you down refer back to it and see no matter what life turns up there is always light at the end of a tunnel, and perhaps if you believe my words of a guardian angel, one watches over you.

It seems some stories have to be told good, bad happy, or sad, people say it's good to write your life story it brings you closure, and yes I'm thankful that for just a short while in my mind whilst writing my story I've lived once more with my mother father, and five beautiful brothers.

My brother Victor after being lost all those years ago has been remembered. If I could I would add music when I tell of my mother, and brothers "The Fields of Gold" springs to my mind by singer-songwriter Sting.

In my story I have been at the top of the world and also brought down to deep despair I have had to relive my personal life remembering its pain like it was only yesterday, there will always be a weight on my shoulders through the life I have led Reading my story you may presume I am a sad kind of person, but no thanks to my children, and brothers along with my Italian family, and friends I have laughed and been happy many times.

I now work in the Liverpool Royal Hospital, and feel it is a worthwhile job; I have built some friendships during my time there, and try to pass on words of comfort to the many sick people who enter the hospital and pass my way.

God only knows what type of person I would have become had life been a little kinder.

Although I can imagine a huge house somewhere in Canada with six brothers and maybe a sister, and their families gathered each Christmas. I have realised being with family and friends is all I need to keep the hurt of the past at bay.

I have tried in my life to make a difference by giving love, and have passed these virtues to my children, likewise, I'm proud to say so have both my brothers. I am far from wealthy, but rich in the knowledge life goes on, and can only get better, and literally as I finish my story great news my deceased brother Danny's daughter has just given birth to a baby boy named Jacob on 06/01/2012 the same day and month as my toddler Brother Russell who was lost back in 1957.

Danny will be looking down at this event as a proud grandfather and overjoyed for his first grandson. I hope you agree that the story of three Brothers who tried their best to be ordinary like the neighbour at the start of my story had said, but through events and memories, we sadly could never quite be.

I can assure you on many a long night with tears smiles, and one finger typing I have told my story true, I have not tried to compete with other stories, but have tried to convey some simple messages, for a short while you have lived my life, in doing so eased the hurt of a life that befell my family, and I hope made you treasure yours.

My sincerest thoughts are that I can look at my sons, and daughter, my brother's children, and our grandchildren, and be proud that my brothers and I kept to the straight and narrow.

Some people have asked me often why I am not mad, how much can one man take, believe me, it would have been easier to have turned to the dark side of life, but what truth could I have written for the love of my Mother, Father Brothers and Children if I had gone down that path.

During childhood, and some of my adult life always being put down and belittled by people who I thought were honest, without guidance I let these people take advantage of my brothers, and this left me thinking at one point in my life that I could not write this story, but thanks to my friend Frank Patten for boosting my lost confidence when I sometimes wanted to give up, I persevered

As a child, Liverpool, and Montreal scared me, but I now know as a man Liverpool people are the salt of the earth, as are many in London Canada Italy in fact, all over the world.

I dedicate this true story to my brothers, myself and our families and all down-to-earth people who understand the pain of life.

What I never mentioned in the book is that I would have loved to have had a sister, but was glad I never, fore, had a sister lead anything like my brothers and my life, for me is unthinkable.

Also, I must mention the much-needed assistance from Andrew Tymms and Bill Tasker for formatting my pictures, two of the nicest people you could meet. Also, with thanks to Ceridwen re- Natasha De Chroustchoff of Geography for her images of places in London.

And a special thank you to my brother's daughter Vicky for her wonderful gesture in arranging our emotional trip to Canada although sad we needed to bring some closure and to make this story complete.

The future is not for any of us to see, so I feel I must try to leave some words of advice hopefully not needed by many good people, just a small reminder, no matter how often you meet your children, grandchildren, parents, brothers, or sisters, mum, or dad, hug them build their confidence, take it from me it means so much, especially in the development of children In writing this story I have found respect from the many people who have read my book and understand what life can throw at you without any warning, they feel I have helped them in some small way to you all thank you for reading my story.

Without a doubt the devil has friends, one of them is in the form of an uncontrolled house fire. It is one of the evillest things that can happen to a family, it creeps silently through your house while you sleep, and shows no mercy.

Thankfully there are now smoke detectors available so check your detectors.

Make sure you have one, advise family and friends to be aware of the pitfalls.

A home should always be a haven for all, unlike the hell which can be seen in pictures at the end of my story.

Again, thank you for reading my story.

I end with words often written and I think well understood in this uncertain world of joy, pain and sorrow. “There but for the Grace of God go I”. “And suffer not the little children” below are pictures and a YouTube film of my brothers and I thank you for reading my story, and through it all I have Lewis, Joey, Reuben and little Vinnie all my grandchildren to date how good is that.

There are pictures and documents plus a YouTube Canadian TV film of our trip to Montreal in the last few pages of my story which I feel have to be added to my story and link well to my story and give factual evidence to all I have written.

My Mother Victoria aged 16 in Montreal just before meeting my father.

Merchant seamen identity photographs. My father at 17 years old

The Aquitania ship my mother left Canada on in 1947 equal in size to the Titanic.

On arrival at my father's home, she would have been dismayed, it was a hovel poorly lit by gas with no electricity. The property a disgrace to the landlord.

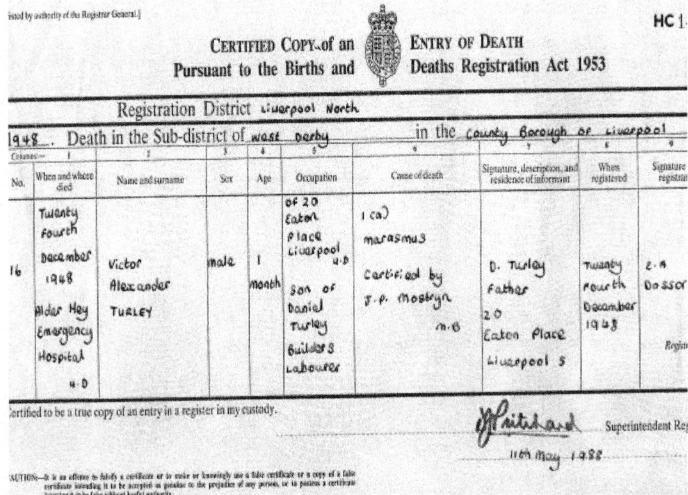

HC 1

CERTIFIED COPY of an ENTRY OF DEATH
Pursuant to the Births and Deaths Registration Act 1953

Registration District Liverpool North

1948. Death in the Sub-district of West Derby in the County Borough of Liverpool

No.	When and where died	Name and surname	Sex	Age	Occupation	Cause of death	Signature, description, and residence of informant	When registered	Signature of registrar
16	Twenty fourth December 1948 Alder Hey Emergency Hospital U.D	Victor Alexander TURLEY	male	1 month	of 20 Eaton Place Liverpool U.D Son of Daniel Turley Builders Labourer	1 (a) marasmus Certified by J.P. Mostyn M.B	D. Turley Father 20 Eaton Place Liverpool 5	Twenty fourth December 1948	E. A. Dossor Registrar

Certified to be a true copy of an entry in a register in my custody.

[signature] Superintendent Registrar

11th May 1988

Victor sadly was not a strong baby the freezing winter, and damp living conditions took their toll, he lived for thirty-eight days dying on Christmas Eve 1948.

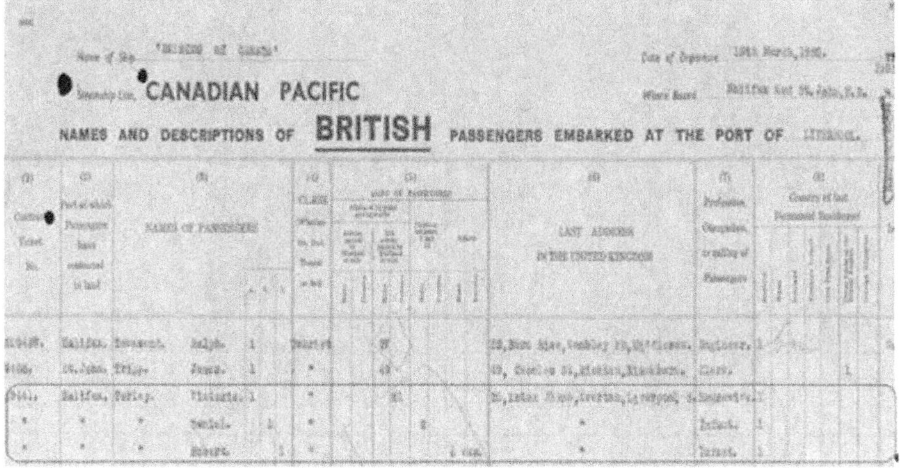

CANADIAN PACIFIC

NAMES AND DESCRIPTIONS OF **BRITISH** PASSENGERS EMBARKED AT THE PORT OF

Shipping tickets dated 15th March 1950.

The Empress of Canada

The fine Empress ship was docked at the pier head in front of the famous Liver Building. "Now a world heritage site" here is where we boarded for Canada.

Mackayville 1952 picture shows my parents Danny and I

Famous Rocket Richard.

Billy Two Rivers, Lived near our home

By December that year, ten years had passed since my mother's marriage, six boys had been born she was now 29 years old. All seemed well for the Turley family.

Une mère et ses deux enfants brûlés vifs à Mackayvil

I was two months from my eighth birthday and could not fully contemplate what dire straits my family now had to face.

LA PRESSE

s autres morts dans un ince

nes enfants
nère brûlés
Mackayville

That morning on the 3rd of December 1957 the press put their versions of events French and English newspapers wrote of my mother's bravery in great detail, of a mother returning to a burning building trying to save her sons. She died with Russell in her arms. Kevin in his pushchair all three so close to the back door.

The Montreal Star

CITY EDITION

FLAMES KILL THREE IN MACKAYVILLE

'Not Enough Hose'

Mother, Two Sons Trapped In Home

Mother, 2 Tots Die As Father Rescues Three

Survivors Of Family Separated

La mort par le feu les a épargnés

La mort par le feu a de nouveau frappé hier. Cette fois, une mère de Mackayville et deux de ses enfants ont péri brulés dans l'incendie de leur maison, tandis que le chef de la famille et trois autres enfants avaient la vie sauve. On voit ici M. Daniel Thurley et ses trois fils qu'il a retirés lui-même des flammes. Madame Thurley, qui avait voulu sauver les deux autres, a péri avec eux. (Voir nouvelle page 6)
(Photo "Mon réal-Matin")

Haunted petrified faces that no dictionary could compete with.

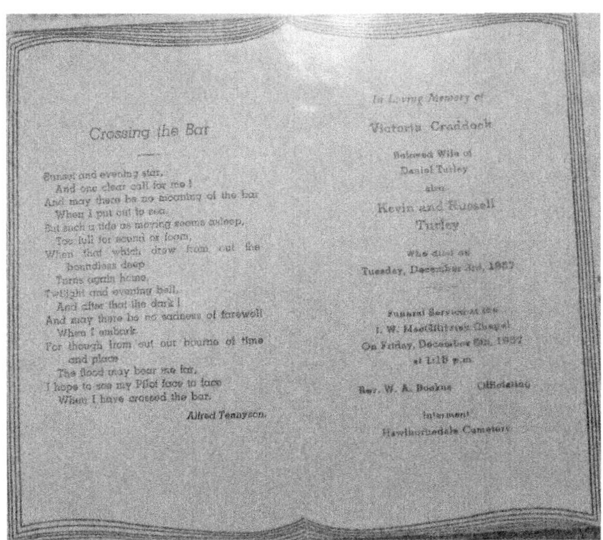

Crossing the Bar

Sunset and evening star,
And one clear call for me!
And may there be no moaning of the bar
When I put out to sea.
But such a tide as moving seems asleep,
Too full for sound or foam,
When that which drew from out the boundless deep
Turns again home.
Twilight and evening bell,
And after that the dark!
And may there be no sadness of farewell
When I embark;
For though from out our bourne of time and place
The flood may bear me far,
I hope to see my Pilot face to face
When I have crossed the bar.

Alfred Tennyson.

In Loving Memory of

Victoria Craddock

Beloved Wife of
Daniel Turley

also

Kevin and Russell
Turley

Who died on
Tuesday, December 3rd, [illegible]

Funeral Services at the
I. W. [illegible] Chapel
On Friday, December [illegible], [illegible]
at 1:15 p.m.

Rev. W. A. Boskus Officiating

Interment
Hawthornedale Cemetery

Three days after the fire my mother and brothers were buried.

'Not Enough Hose'

Mother, Two Sons Trapped In Home

A mother and two of her five sons died early yesterday when fire destroyed their home in a wood and tar-paper duplex house in Mackayville.

The deaths brought to 24 the number of persons who have lost their lives in fires in Quebec province since Oct. 1.

The father, Dan Turley, gathered three other children and led them to the street in their pyjamas in near-zero temperatures.

Victims were Mrs. Turley, 28; Russell, 4; and Kevin, five months. Mr. Turley rescued Daniel, 10; Robert, 8; and Michael, 5.

The Turley home was burned to the foundations. The other half of the single-storey building, containing the apartment of L. Vincent, was heavily damaged.

Told Wife to Leave By Back Door

Mr. Turley, a crane operator, said he was awakened at 5.10 a.m.

blaze with a 1,200 gallon capacity tank truck which ran out of water twice and had to be refilled from the nearby hydrant, each trip taking 10 to 15 minutes.

"Three water trucks arrived just after 5.30 a.m. from Croyden and Jacques Cartier and thanks to these we managed to check the blaze before it reached adjoining houses," the chief said.

Not enough hose such a shame.

LA CROIX-ROUGE AIDE LES SURVIVANTS — Après qu'
incendie eut pris la vie de sa femme et de deux de ses cinq fi
M. Daniel Turley, de Mackayville, s'est tourné vers la Croi
Rouge pour lui demander de l'aide. La Société dépêcha sur l
lieux Mme Dora Beveridge du service de secours aux sinistr
et Mme Marcelle Ryan du détachement féminin. La Société
fourni aux sinistrés un abri temporaire, des vêtements, de
nourriture et des couvertures. On voit, ici, M. Daniel Turley
ses trois fils, Daniel, 10 ans, Robert, 8 ans, et Michel, 5 a

My brothers' father and I being helped by the Red Cross.

LES CORPS RETIRES DES DECOMBRES -- Les sapeurs se penchent sur les pauvre victimes qu'ils ont pu retirer des décombres fumantes, une heure après le commencement d l'incendie. La mère est morte, rapporte-t-on, en tentant de sauver ses enfants. (Phot "Montréal-Matin")

Shocked firefighters with large canvas being placed over my Mother, and Brothers.

TRANS-CANADA-AIRLINES
23RD APRIL 1958

4 months later and we were sent from all we had known

BOYS FLY TO NEW HOME IN BRITAIN

Mother Died In Fire

LIVERPOOL AUNT

MONTREAL, Wednesday.

Three small boys, whose mother and two brothers died in a fire here last December, are due in London to-day to live with British relatives.

Their widowed father, British - born crane driver Daniel Turley, who put them on a plane here last night, is staying in Canada.

His three surviving sons, Daniel aged 10, Robert aged 8, and Michael aged 5, will be met at London Airport by their father's sister, Mrs. Eva Morris, of Liverpool. The boys will be split among relatives.

Their mother and two younger brothers died on December 8 when fire swept their home in suburban Mackayville.

—Reuter.

LIVERPOOL Echo, Wednesday
APRIL 23 1958

Without previous knowledge of events you may take it we were about to embark on a holiday, this was a far cry from the truth.

Liverpool Aunt Meets Orphans

Three brothers from Canada with their aunt, Mrs. Evan Morris, of Liverpool, who met them on arrival at London Airport to-day. Their mother and two of their brothers, died in a fire at their home in Mackayville, Montreal, last December and their father sent them home to relatives in Britain. See also story on Page 4).

We were taken to Eaton Place the property my mother had left behind eight years earlier, and split amongst relatives.

My aunt Liz was married to George they had five kids Danny their eldest son was serving in the British Army, the King's Regiment. He boxed, and played football for his regiment, and was fortunate to play a friendly game against the England World Just before the 1966 tournament started, he's next to Roger hunt.

Together for one rare day as children thanks to Aunt Violet. left to right Danny Michael, and Robert

Michael in the middle during his stay with Aunt Uncle and Cousin David. During Michael's first months back with his, he was top of the class at school what he may have achieved is now unknown thanks to evil May's tactics.

The cold tenements were May ruled and ruined Michaels and my life and yet the children in the photo look so happy, but sadly not Michael or I.

The Hercules pub in Holloway It's where I met my 1st wife Linda.

I found a job with Islington council in this nice old building, built in 1931.

My son Justin and I.

Mitch and Danny on my wedding day.

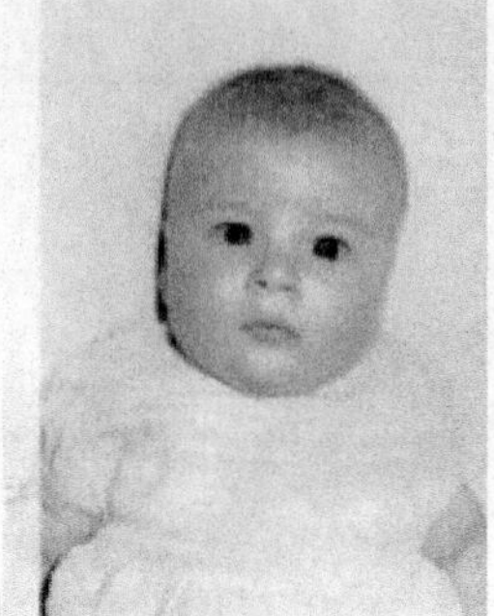
Justin

"Young man you're now the father of a baby boy", "you can see him now."

My brothers would watch me play; here I am wearing number 11.

On Danny's wedding day, he moved to Trowbridge Mitch settled in Liverpool.

My family with Lello Sabatini and their family.

Michael's daughter Vicky, Michael (left).

.

PILGRIMAGE TO A TRAGIC PAST

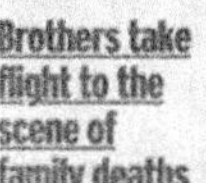

Brothers take flight to the scene of family deaths

A group of Vicky's staff members felt so strongly about our story they decided to ring the Liverpool Echo newspaper.

I realised on that cold morning we were recapturing a childhood memory that we had missed in our time away from Montreal.

Mother and brother's resting place.

Quest accomplished no longer a pauper's grave

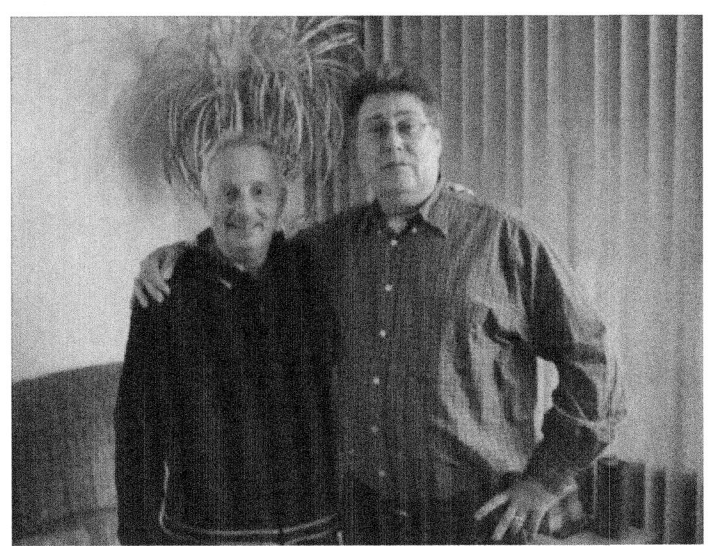

MICHAEL AND RONALD NELSON.

It was then the gentleman we now know as Ronald said as if just waking up to reality "One moment I will phone my brother", "He was eighteen at the time of the fire perhaps, he can help".

We left De Gaulle Street following Ronald to his brother's house, after a drive of about thirty minutes we pulled into a double-fronted driveway, there stood a huge pebble-built Canadian-looking house; we were all greeted by a smartly dressed gentleman who introduced himself as Claude.

Mrs. Nelson Claude and Ronald's mother the keeper of our past for over 44 years. She always felt we would return one day which was the reason she kept all the newspaper cuttings. A very special lady, thank you, Danny Robert and Michael

Canada Now news reporter and cameraman

PHOTO TAKEN BY
NELSON FAMILY 1950'S
DE GAULLE STREET
MONTREAL

BACKGROUND OF PHOTO
TURLEY FAMILY HOME
1525 DE GAULLE STREET
PICTURED BROTHER DANNY
LEANING ON GATE

HOUSE IN BACKGROUND
1525 DE GAULLE STREET
BROTHER DANNY LEANING
ON THE GATE
MONTREAL CANADA

To our surprise we received a wonderful photograph from Claude Nelson taken from his family house back in 1950s Mackayville, revealing our house before the fire. The Nelson family picture our house in the background, Danny standing by the gate of our home, the windows beautifully dressed by my mother.

Also, with the picture was a hand-written note expressing their heartfelt feelings at our visit penned by Ronald Nelson who told us he rarely wrote in English. He describes his family's feelings.

Written thought of Ronald Nelso after our visit 2002 CANADA

"The strangest thing happened yesterday
Three men, three brothers came into our home
With smile on their faces and tears into their eyes
They came from far away in distance and much farther away in time
They came into the present, three men from the past
Searching for a missing link in their life
Knocking at our door for answers
Three French Canadians, three *Québécois*
With pictures in their head and in their hands
Shared those sad memories with them
Tried to give them a little something of what they were searching for
Brought more tears to theirs eyes and, maybe, relief in their hearts
Three nice men came and went away and I didn't slept well that night
My head filled with their sorrows and with our past
What else is their to say, we tried our best to help
My wife is very happy to have been there for them
We wish to these brothers and the people they love
All the happiness that can be live on this earth
And a very special "Thank you" to the lady who made their dream come to reality"

Mme Georgette Paquette-Nelson. Our dear mother. (6 ly 1915 / 16 February 2002)

She's the one who kept all those documents that you have now.

She always was very afraid of fire, I think you know at least one good reason for that.

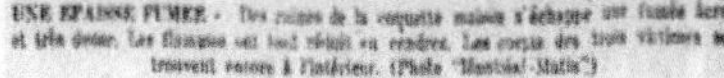

UNE EPAISSE FUMEE - Des ruines de la coquette maison s'échappe une fumée âcre et très dense. Les flammes ont tout réduit en cendres. Les corps des trois victimes se trouvent encore à l'intérieur. (Photo "Montréal-Matin")

LES RUINES -- Hier matin, au lever du soleil, il ne restait que des ruines. Comme on le voit par cette photo, toute la maison de bois recouverte d'imitation de brique a été détruite par les flammes. (Photo "Montréal-Matin", par Bernard [illegible])

Sad remains of a happy home

Mitch (left) Danny (middle) Robert (right)

Thank you for reading our story.

If you would like to watch the Canadian TV documentary please google "The Turley Brothers Canada 2002" which is located on YouTube.

Printed in Great Britain
by Amazon